Turning
Premiums
Into
Profits

How you can simultaneously build equity and
reduce your total cost of risk utilizing your business
insurance program

by

David R. Leng
CPCU, CIC, CBWA, CWCA, CRM

White Publishing

Publisher: White Publishing, Norwell, MA
Editor: Steve White

This book contains information about insurance and coverage. The information is not intended as a substitute for insurance, legal, or financial advice from an appropriately qualified professional and should not be treated as such. If you have any specific questions about any insurance matters, you should consult an appropriately qualified professional.

First Edition: November 2017
Printed in the United States of America
ISBN: [9781973152682]

To my good friend Bob Seltzer, you were one of a kind.

Even at 68, you proved you are never too old to learn and try new things, and use them to make a difference in someone's life.

Table of Contents

Section 1 – Understanding Captives

Section 2 – Improving Captive Results

Table of Contents

Foreword

As business owners, we face risks (threats) to our business every day. Plus, to run a successful business there are a lot of hats that must be worn. Whether we wear them all ourselves, or have others that help us; overseeing payroll, HR, production, distribution, safety, and the ever-changing OSHA and other governmental regulations that need complied with, are enough to make anyone's head spin.

In addition to all of those, having competition also squeeze our bottom-lines makes it imperative that we diligently maintain a certain level of frugalness when it comes to costs. And that is a hard-fought battle when it comes to the specter of rapidly increasing and often insurmountable insurance costs.

Increased costs have seemingly always been a trait of traditional insurance products. No matter how judicious we are in trying to control our company's risk factors, it always seems that at renewal time the needle invariably points north. You work hard to make your risks goes down, and yet, some insurance company underwriter seems to want to push your insurance costs up. On any business owner's frustration meter, I am sure this is definitely an 11.

So, one day, somebody who knows a whole lot more about managing risks and insurance than I do suggests that there is an alternative, one they call Captives. And what sounds like a P.O.W movie suddenly brightens up the insurance landscape. It's proverbially like somebody throwing a lifeline to keep us from fiscally drowning, one that we would be foolhardy not to latch on to.

We learned that by utilizing a **Captive Insurance Program** as an alternative to traditional insurance, we can use a type of self-insurance that allows us, in essence, to join with other like-minded, well run and safe companies, to form our own insurance company and, now get this, pretty much *insure ourselves*. Not only do we gain operational transparency, coverage flexibility, greater control, reduced costs and increased cash-flow, any profits from our insurance program is returned to us and not sent off to the insurance company's shareholders. Plus, our captive premiums are based on the quality of our business, and not on the general insurance marketplace rates. For us, it's the definition of a win-win.

For the same reason you probably wouldn't perform surgery on yourself, you need a talented insurance professional to really get into the nuts and bolts of how Captives works, and if it is right path for your company to take. I have known David Leng for years, and during that time have trusted him to steer our company in the right direction regarding our risks and insurance. And if David has the knowledge and the resources to put everything you need to know about Captives in the pages of this book, then I would suggest it's a book well worth reading. Don't wait to do so, as waiting for your insurance renewal date will probably cost you more in terms of money and headaches.

Bob Monpara,
President – MBPJ Corporation

Acknowledgements

I would like to thank Jon Kirssin for his education and insights on 831(b) Enterprise Risk Captives. John has worked closely with me and a number of my clients by helping them to implement appropriate alternative risk financing strategies for over 10 years. Jon D. Kirssin is the Principal of CFMC, Inc., a captive and general insurance consulting and management company formed in July 2001. Prior to founding CFMC, John was involved in managing captives for PMA Insurance Company.

I would also like to thank Dennis Silvia for his guidance and assistance in managing our group and agency captives for over 10 years. Dennis Silvia the captive manager for the Keystone Insurers Group, and has been the president of Cedar Consulting LLC, in Chagrin Falls, OH since 2005. Prior to that, he spent five years as Director of Group Captive Programs for CNA Insurance Co. in Chicago. In the decade preceding, Dennis served as Vice President, Captive Products for National Interstate Insurance Company in Richfield, OH. Dennis also serves on the faculty of the International Center for Captive Insurance Education (ICCIE)

Turning Premiums Into Profits

Introduction

When it comes to controlling and managing your insurance program, and most likely with you focusing on reducing your premiums, the odds are you will probably agree with at least a few, if not all, of the following statements:

- *The insurance companies take more of your money than they pay out in claims on your behalf.*
- *It takes a lot of time to shop your insurance, and you still don't receive results you are satisfied with.*
- *Transitioning between insurance agents is painful, and between insurance companies even more so.*
- *There always seems to be something that gets missed when you make a change. And that "something" always comes back to haunt you.*
- *Insurance agents do not really understand what your business is and what your needs are.*
- *You do not fully understand the insurance system.*
- *Insurance companies don't seem to listen to you when it comes to paying your claims.*
- *You do not like to be blindsided by a large premium increase.*
- *The hard and soft insurance marketplace pricing makes it challenging to properly budget.*
- *The insurance industry is not very transparent.*
- *You feel the insurance company has too much control, especially when it comes to how they manage and settle your claims.*
- *There appears to be a lack of creativity when it comes to dealing with your business' risks.*
- *That feeling of being overcharged leaves you yearning for more cost-effective options.*

So how do you end this frustrating cycle of purchasing insurance that leaves you wanting more?
IT IS SIMPLE, JUST READ ON...

Over my 30-plus years as a speaker and an Outsourced Risk Manager, I have interviewed hundreds of business owners, business leaders and executives, and they have all expressed the frustrations I have just outlined. They have also lamented about the amount of time, energy and/or money they have spent dealing with their insurance program.

So why do you, as a successful business owner, keep doing the same things over and over when it comes to managing your insurance program? Only you can answer that question. But you can take some comfort in knowing that you are not alone.

When you look at the amount of money you have wasted on your insurance program, money you could have used to achieve a specific goal within your company, money that could have been used personally, money that could have built equity, how can you not feel frustrated? Think of the amount of time you have frittered away trying to obtain bids or quotes on your insurance program, only to fall short of the results you wanted. And by doing so, you now realize that this time could have been better spent focusing on growing and running your company.

Why do you feel this way?

The answer is really very simple; the insurance industry has taught employers how to purchase insurance but in a way that can best be described as clunky and confusing. You experience it every year, particularly 90-120 days prior to your insurance renewal. This is the time when it seems like insurance agents come out of the woodwork asking to quote your insurance, only to promise much and deliver little.

This is where you are dropping the ball:

- By thinking that being attractive to all the insurance agents calling you to quote your insurance (who simply want a commission from selling you policies) is the same as being *truly* attractive to all insurance companies, and therefore **assuming insurance companies will provide you with a premium commensurate with your risk.**

- By wanting, *instead of demanding,* a better way!

And there is a better, more successful way to manage your insurance costs. Insurance is your way of transferring your *risk* of the unknown to an insurance company in exchange for a known amount of money, commonly known as a *premium*. Through your strong focus on safety and your corporate culture, you have come to a point where you have become very attractive to insurance companies and they are offering you *their* best premiums. But in the end, *their premium is still too much.*

Think of it another way, the efforts and focus on safety that has made you attractive to insurance companies is allowing those insurance companies to take your money (premium) so that they can take on the risks and pay the claims of other businesses that are not as focused on those traits as you are. And, your money also goes to benefit their shareholders. *So why allow your efforts to benefit others?*

This is why businesses are rapidly turning to Alternative Risk Financing Insurance Marketplace…

If you are paying over $100,000 annually in workers' compensation, general liability, and auto insurance premiums combined, or insuring more than 20 employees for health insurance, you can break this costly cycle and gain more control over your insurance costs. Alternative risk financing is when a business does not purchase traditional guaranteed cost insurance policies, but instead purchases insurance where they take on some risk to get potential rewards. For clarification, there is more insurance premiums invested by businesses in the alternative risk financing market than you realize, with the use of Group Captives being the most popular of the alternative risk financing programs being used.

Captives are not a new concept; they have been around for over 100 years. From around 1,000 captives in 1980, there are now over

7,000, according to a September 2014 report by Conning Research & Consulting. In fact, there has been more than a 35% increase in captives in the past 10 years as business owners become more sophisticated and demand better use of their capital. As a result, more and more businesses have turned to captives.

This book is divided into two sections:

In the first section, you will learn about the world of insurance captives, and how to take advantage of their significantly lower insurance costs structures. You will also discover the potential financial and estate benefits of captives, and obtain the ability to take control of your insurance program.

In the second section, the focus is on improving the profitability and results of your captive. We will explore the areas of Risk Management, Safety Culture, Claims Management, Human Capital and Benchmarking your results.

Yes, in the captive world you are able to take control of your insurance program, just as you control your business. In other words, instead of focusing on your insurance costs as an expense, you will now be able to view it as investing in a profit center that builds wealth for you.

———————

The Insurance Marketplace

Business leaders who successfully manage their risks eventually ask the question: ***What should I do when the insurance companies continually takes more of our money than they pay out on our behalf?***

Face it, your efforts and focus on safety, the very attributes that have made you attractive to insurance companies, are allowing those same insurance companies to make an underwriting profit off your business. In essence, that underwriting profit is excess premiums, and it allows the insurance company to take on the risks and pay the claims of businesses that are not as focused as you are. Plus, your excess premiums go to benefit their shareholders in the form of insurance company profits.

Then you realize your situation has gotten worse when the insurance industry experiences a "hard market," a time period when the insurance industry seeks to increase overall rates due to inadequately charging companies with poor claims experience enough premium. When better performing companies like yours cannot offset the losses of poorer performing businesses, the insurance companies still need to be profitable for their shareholders, so they must increase *everyone's* rates - including yours. This is why businesses continue to turn to the alternative risk financing market.

Why is alternative risk financing so popular?

When you have a strong safety focus and a great corporate culture, whether buying insurance outright for your organization or buying excess coverage if you are self-insured, it typically comes down to financing your risk and purchasing some form of insurance. To answer the question as to why alternative risk financing programs, particularly group captives, have become so popular, it is necessary to review all of the programs available to you, so you can see what the options are.

There are multiple types of programs available to transfer risk to an insurance company for a premium. We will go through a number of the programs in some detail as well as summarize and provide highlights, with advantages and disadvantages of each. To include all the details associated with each form of insurance program outside of captives would be a lengthy book indeed.

The programs range from the highest cost for you to insure your risk down to the lowest cost. Ranking them in that order, starting with guaranteed cost as the costliest, we then move on to dividend, retrospectively-rated, high-deductible, captives. And, finally, the lowest-cost program, which is typically found with self-insurance programs.

		Plan
Highest ‐ ‐ ‐ ‐ ‐ ‐ ‐ **Lowest**		Guaranteed Cost
		Dividend
		Retrospectively Rated
		High-Deductible
		Captive
		Self-Insurance

Each of these programs has pluses and minuses. Ultimately, you must make a decision based on the cost-benefit analysis for your company. You need to determine which program best suits you, your needs, your cash flow and your financial position, in order to pay the lowest net costs possible for your insurance program.

Guaranteed Cost

A Guaranteed Cost program is just what its name implies. You pay a certain premium based on the underwriter's perception of your risk. The only variation comes at the end of the year when the insurance company conducts its year-end premium audit. There is no real risk to you as an organization, outside of retentions or deductibles per claim, which are very small. The main advantage of this program is that you are able to budget exactly how much you will spend for your insurance for that year.

The reason Guaranteed Cost is the highest is because insurance companies are in business to make a profit for their shareholders. Therefore, they are going to determine the amount that they want to charge for the potential losses for your organization, based on what the underwriter perceives as your risks. The underwriter is then going to add their expense ratio (cost of marketing acquisition, policy underwriting and service, and agent commissions), the insurance company profit, and then add in for a margin of error. Typically, insurance company expense ratios are in the 25-35% range. After adding in profit and margin of error, you are looking at 35-50% of your premium being used for expenses not associated with paying any claims on your behalf.

To determine the premium of your insurance program, the insurance companies will ultimately want to calculate your policy premium in order for them to achieve an expected loss ratio of 30-50%. They will calculate the premium of an employer they perceive to be a better risk closer to an expected 50% loss ratio. Those they perceive to be more of a risk will be priced higher at an expected 30-35% loss ratio. To understand loss ratio, you must determine your yearly average claim total using the average of all your claim costs for the last five years. A 50% loss ratio premium could be calculated by doubling your yearly average. A 30% loss ratio premium could be roughly calculated by tripling your yearly average.

Also, "hard market" or "soft market" condition influences underwriters as well. In a "hard market," where buying insurance is a little more difficult and rates are going up, there is pressure on the underwriters for higher rates. The underwriters will err on the conservative side and judge a risk poorer and push more towards the

30% loss ratio, resulting in a higher premium. In a "soft market," an underwriter may be more aggressive and a little more forgiving, thus underwriting to a higher loss ratio, resulting in a lower premium. As you can see, they are taking all of your expected losses and significantly marking them up and adjusting them based on the perception of your risk.

For example, if the underwriter expected to pay out $120,000 a year in claims, depending upon their perception of your risk, and if it is a "hard" or "soft" market, they may charge you anywhere from $240,000-$400,000 for your policy.

Dividend Program

The Dividend Program is nothing more than a guaranteed cost insurance policy with a return of premium dividend potential. Based on the overall loss ratio (losses divided by your final premium), you may expect to receive a return of a portion of your of premium, typically one year to two years following the expiration of your policy. The dividend may be anywhere from zero dividend on poor performance, to perhaps 10%, 15%, or even potentially 20% for a good or outstanding performance.

Many insurance companies like to tout their biggest potential dividend, which might be 30% or 35%. However, you would need zero losses ($0 paid *or reserved*) to attain the highest advertised dividend payout. If you have one dollar of loss (or reserve), you will have some percentage other than a 0.00% loss ratio and you will drop down to a much lower percentage.

Interestingly enough, insurance companies do tend to charge a little extra premium for policies with a dividend associated with them because they know that ultimately they will have to pay out, or could pay out, a significant portion of the premium in a dividend. This way they can maintain profitability.

The exception might be a group dividend program based on, for example, an association or a specific group of businesses. The insurance company is then able to spread the risk over more policies and therefore have a much more stable outcome from a profit standpoint. They would not necessarily need to inflate the premium of each policy to pay for the dividend.

It is important to note that the amount the underwriter may choose to inflate your premium by may be anywhere from a relatively small to an amount larger than you might think, so it is wise to ask what your premium would be with the dividend, and what your premium would be without the dividend. This way you can compare and decide if the difference in premium is worth waiting for the potential dividend.

When it comes to declaring a dividend, the insurance company will want to allow for "claim development," which allows the adjuster more time so they have a better idea as to the severity of the injury and potential claim costs. Therefore, the dividend calculation date, or dividend valuation date, will typically be anywhere from 12-24 months after your policy expiration date. You may also want to know that the insurance company will not pay any dividend on "fees or assessments," such as terrorism charges, state assessments or taxes, expense constant, etc.

An important item of note is that dividends are not guaranteed, and are subject to that insurance company's board of directors' approval. Although it is extremely rare not to be paid, there is the potential for an insurance company to choose not to pay out a dividend even if "earned," especially if the insurance company is having financial difficulties.

Retrospectively-Rated Program

The Retrospectively-Rated Programs take this risk-reward proposition a step further. A Retrospectively-Rated Program is just what it says. After your program period is over, the insurance company will then retroactively determine your final premium. They will look backwards at what the total amount of your claims were and then calculate your final premium based on total amount of the losses, subject to both a minimum and maximum premium.

The insurance company will calculate the final premium charge each year until such time that the retrospective contract terminates. The retrospective contract could contain a three, four, five, six, or seven-year termination period. Most will be longer in length so that all claims close and the insurance company is confident that there is no possibility of a future claim reopening or being brought to light.

On the other hand, a shorter term may seem appealing, but then your final premium will be based on total claims, including reserves that have yet to be paid, or may never be paid.

Your standard premium, which is the basis for the Retrospectively-Rated Program calculation, is determined much like a guaranteed-cost premium, which is based on the perception of your risk. The difference is that a Retrospectively-Rated premium does not include a premium size discount and typically carries a slightly higher premium to start with as compared to a guaranteed cost policy.

The best way to understand a Retrospectively-Rated program is to go through an example. In this example, we will pretend your standard premium is $250,000 (line C in Diagram), and you will have had $60,000 in losses.

Retrospectively-Rated Program Diagram

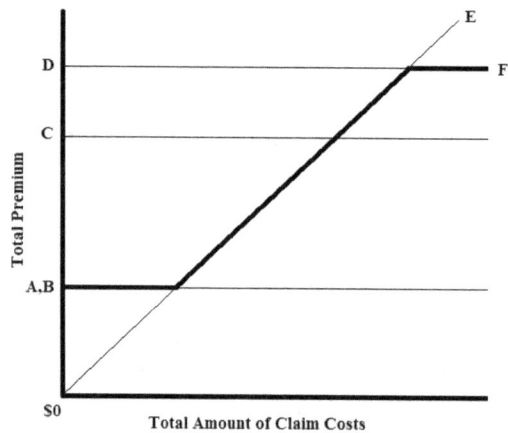

First, the insurance company will have a Basic Premium Factor (line A in diagram), or base charge, which is their expense ratio, profit, and "reinsurance" if your losses exceed the formula's maximum rating ability. In this example, we will use 40% or $100,000 to cover their expenses and what they view as reinsurance or excess insurance should you have a horrendous loss year.

The insurance company will then add to the basic premium charge the $60,000 in losses that the insurance company paid out on your behalf, including reserves. In addition, there are usually two multipliers that are applied to those losses: Loss Conversion Factor, to pay for the costs of the claims department to adjust your claim and also to allow for development of the claim as claim costs typically go up over time; and a State Premium Tax Multiplier, to cover the associated state premium taxes. Line E in the diagram represents the final calculation of the loss portion of the premium determination.

Be aware that some insurance companies will also add in a third multiplier for IBNR (Incurred But Not Reported losses) for the potential that a claim may be reported years later. Now keep in mind that most states have statutes of limitations on how late a claim can be reported, but this charge would be in the Retrospectively-Rated Program contract and may be charged well after the statute of limitations is over.

Let us use a Loss Conversion Factor of 10% (1.10) and a Tax Multiplier of 5% (1.05). In this example, if you take your losses of $60,000 and multiply them by 1.10, and then by 1.05, you come up with a claims charge of $69,300. We will not use IBNR in this example, as it is not a normal charge.

As you can see, your final premium will be your claims plus surcharges, plus your base charge. However, that is a little too unstable, or too unpredictable, on both ends. So the insurance company typically will include a minimum percentage and a maximum percentage.

The insurance company will have a Minimum Premium Factor (line B in diagram), which is normally equal to that of the Basic Premium Factor. Occasionally, I have seen some policies that had higher minimum premium factors. Insurance companies use higher minimums when they want to use the Retrospectively-Rated Program more as a tool to collect additional premium from a business rather than to reward them for being a better risk.

On the other end of the spectrum would be a Maximum Premium Factor (line D in diagram). This would be used to determine the most you would have to pay for a program year. It might be 125% of your standard premium or even higher.

When structured properly, a Retrospectively-Rated Program will yield a lower net premium cost to you as a business. Keep in mind, whether you want a bigger reward or a lower Minimum Premium

Factor, the insurance company will typically push the Maximum Premium Factor higher to have the upper amount capped. When structuring your Retrospectively-Rated Program, you will want your Minimum Premium Factor to be as low as possible, making sure that the Maximum Premium Factor does not make the risk-reward decision too unpalatable.

For this example, we will use a Minimum Premium Factor equal to your Basic Premium Factor of 40% (0.40), and a Maximum Premium Factor of 125% (1.25). Your Basic Premium Factor is $100,000, and your losses result in a premium charge of $69,300, thus your final calculated premium would be $169,300. So in this example, as your total calculated premium is less than your Standard Premium, you would receive a refund of $71,700 in premium. If you had $0 in losses, you would receive a refund of $150,000. However, if your claim costs exceeded $129,870, you would owe additional premium over the initial $250,000 paid in. In this example, once your total claim costs exceeded $182,247, you would hit the Maximum Premium Factor and would owe an additional $62,500 in premium. The bold line F in the diagram represents the final premium you will pay based on the calculation of your losses.

You can reap the rewards of having your house in order and achieving better results by moving towards the alternative funding programs of retrospective, high deductible, captive, and self-insurance. And by doing so, you can reduce your cost of insurance far greater than with guaranteed cost or dividends.

You can see the advantage of significantly lower premiums and the flexibility of the program. The disadvantages of this program include uncertainty surrounding final premium, and the premium paid may be higher than guaranteed cost if you do not control your losses.

Unfortunately, Retrospectively-Rated Programs have earned a bad reputation because insurance companies typically present Retrospectively-Rated Programs to businesses that do not have their house in order and thus experience significant losses. The reason insurance companies do this is to collect the extra premium to offset the losses that have occurred. In essence, the insurance companies use the Retrospectively-Rated Program to provide them with additional premium. Because they simply cannot price the premium high enough to their liking, and cannot use a high enough rate or add enough surcharges to the guaranteed cost program as they would prefer, they use a Retrospectively-Rated Program to accomplish it.

At times I have seen Retrospectively-Rated Programs used with poorly managed risks with minimums of only 80% to 90% (0.80-0.90) and utilizing maximums as high as 150% to 220% (1.50-2.20). As you see, a Retrospectively-Rated Program can be used by insurance companies as a tool to collect more premiums by creating a skewed risk-reward with the advantage in favor of the insurance company.

On the other hand, these programs are not frequently proposed to businesses that do have their houses in order. Most insurance agents do not truly understand the Retrospectively-Rated Program and therefore cannot explain it to an executive well enough for that person to become comfortable with the program. Also, insurance companies do not readily offer them to well-run businesses as the insurance company would obtain more premiums from the business owner using the guaranteed cost policy.

It is very important to understand how loss levels or claim total dollars spent equate to what premium you ultimately pay. That way you can make an intelligent financial decision regarding risk-reward.

High-Deductible

High-deductible is the next step just before you would go into a captive or self-insured program. In this program, you accept a high-deductible per claim, typically a minimum of $25,000 or $50,000 per claim or higher, with the possibility of $100,000, $250,000, $300,000 or even half a million dollars or more per claim (see A in diagram below). To prevent too much financial uncertainty caused by a high frequency of injuries with a high-deductible program, you may also have an aggregate-deductible amount (see B in diagram below). This aggregate-deductible enables you to have some maximum cost certainty. The aggregate might be two to five times the amount of the per-claim deductible, or even more, depending upon the premium size of your company.

It is up to the underwriter and the insurance company to determine exactly what this aggregate deductible amount might be. They then determine the amounts that exceed this per- claim deductible for an individual claim, or when the total of all your deductibles exceeds your aggregate maximum deductible, then the insurance company pays (see the diagram below).

High-Deductible Program Diagram

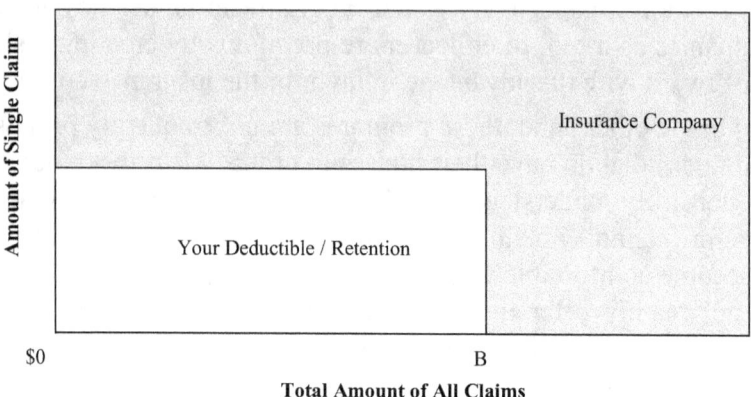

Total Amount of All Claims

Through these high deductibles you will find yourself paying most, if not all of your claim costs. You are purchasing excess coverage from an insurance company for very large claims or very bad years. You receive a substantial premium reduction through a large credit that is applied to your policy in order to reduce the insurance premium portion you pay. In essence, a high deductible is not much different than self-insurance, except you do not have to deal with all of the state regulatory issues of self-insuring. All functions and services provided by the insurance company are marked up for their profit.

Much like you saw in the Retrospectively-Rated Program, the insurance company is going to mark up the claims to cover claims handling expenses, development factors, taxes and possibly fees. Read your contract carefully to understand exactly what they are adding to each claim dollar spent on your behalf, including reserves. The downside to the High-Deductible Program is the fact that you as an organization, from a tax standpoint, can only deduct as an insurance expense the amount of premium that you pay, and the amount you pay for actual claims paid. You will not be able to deduct the reserves you must set aside and pay to the insurance company for reserves (potential claims payout).

Each insurance company decides if they want to collect the deductible payment for both paid and reserves, or if it is based simply on paid claims. You may also have to set aside either a letter of credit or supply the insurance company with a cash deposit or letter of credit to collateralize and guarantee you will pay promptly any invoice for claim payments the insurance company makes on your behalf.

Self-Insurance

Although Self-Insurance will typically have a lower total cost of risk over a captive, we will jump ahead to Self-Insurance before we return to captives in the next chapter to close out this overview.

Even with Self-Insurance, you still have to typically purchase excess or stop loss (reinsurance coverage) to protect your organization when you have a significantly large claim or a series of larger claims. As an organization you should not assume unlimited risk. You normally purchase your reinsurance as your safety net so that you will know what your maximum annual liability will be (see B in diagram) and for any one claim (see A in diagram).

Self-Insurance Program Diagram

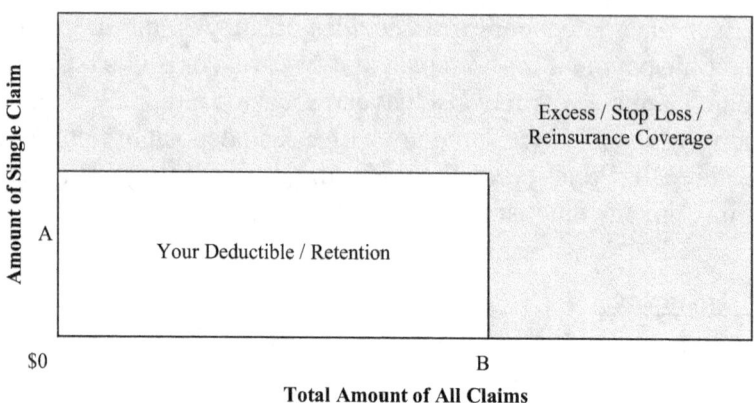

When you Self-Insure you must file with the state insurance department and receive approval. Most states will even tell you what reinsurance to purchase, stating the per claim and aggregate retention amounts that must be used. You must also hire a third-party administrator to legally adjudicate your claims unless you have a licensed adjuster on staff. You will need to set aside monies, also known as reserves, to pay your claims and future claims. You must also have your program audited by an independent auditor to evaluate and make sure you have properly funded your program.

As I mentioned with high deductibles, you will be able to deduct for tax purposes your excess premium and all the fees that you pay for claims administration and actuary services, as well as the actual amount you pay for claims. However, you will not be able to deduct the amounts that you set aside for reserves.

Because you self-administer more of the process, the cost structure of managing Self-Insured is lower than in a captive, and much lower than high-deductible programs. Therefore, your overall Self-Insurance will traditionally lower your net cost over time more than a captive, high deductible or guaranteed cost.

As you can see, the more risk you take on yourself, the lower your cost of risk, such as your insurance cost. However, never take that huge step into the alternative funding, or any change beyond guaranteed cost, unless you conduct an analysis and *fully* understand your risk-reward. You also need to understand the cash flow implications and collateral requirements of each model, so that ultimately you achieve your goal of dramatically reducing your costs.

———————

What is a Captive?

Simply put, a captive is an insurance company. It receives premiums in exchange for providing coverage for the risks they are insuring or protecting and they pay claims. But the biggest difference between a captive and an insurance company is that although the insurance company can work with individuals and businesses directly, at large, a captive cannot sell insurance to the public. It can only manage and transact business with the members of those captive or other insurance companies. A captive identifies what the risks are, provides coverage and writes policies, sets premiums, and determines who they can and cannot insure. As you can see – it acts like any other insurance company.

Captives have been around for hundreds of years, dating back to ship owners that would share in the risks of voyages. In the late 1800's, protective indemnity clubs were created. Although captive growth was slow, they saw a significant growth, particularly in the 1980's when a significant hard market hit, making insurance hard to obtain and very expensive to purchase, which led to financial federal law reform. Today captives are exploding. Over the last 20 years the numbers have doubled. With over 7,000 worldwide, and more than a 35% growth since 2006, captives are the most popular of the alternative risk financing options.

Insurance companies must be initially formed, licensed, filed to do business and approved by a governmental body, and are often referred to their place of domicile. Or in the case of statutorily required coverage of Workers' Compensation and Auto Liability, by the state your employees or vehicles reside. Captives are being formed, or domiciled, both inside and outside of the United States. Outside, some of the biggest are Bermuda, Cayman Islands, and the

British Virgin Islands. Inside the United States, the leading domiciles are Vermont, Hawaii, South Carolina, and Arizona – and the numbers of states are growing.

Captives are growing in numbers because business owners are tired of the traditional insurance marketplace, where insurance companies determine what their risk profile is and what the insurance company expects to pay in claims, and *then* try to price their insurance to either a 30% hard market loss ratio, or a 50% soft market loss ratio. Loss ratio is your claims over a three-to-five-year period divided by the premiums you paid during that same period. Basically, business owners are tired of insurance companies charging them double or triple what is expected to be paid out on their behalf.

Either way, insurance companies expect to pay out far less than what they take in. And they make money in two ways: Underwriting Profit and Cash-Flow Investment Income.

Underwriting Profit

The insurance company charges premiums to their insured's (clients). From the premiums they receive they pay operational expenses, as well as pay for the claims of their clients. When an insurance company collects more in premiums than they pay out in expenses or claims, they make an underwriting profit. This underwriting profit is why most business owners that control their claims feel like the insurance industry takes advantage of them; the insurance companies collect more in premium than they pay out on their behalf.

Cash-flow Investment Income

The other way insurance companies make money is from cash-flow. This is why people like Warren Buffett are in the insurance business. For example, the insurance company charges and collects a business dollar premium on day one. We also know that the claims rarely happen on day one. They happen days and even months later. When claims do happen, they take a while to get reported. When they do get reported, they take a while longer to be settled. Insurance companies have the benefit of collecting that dollar premium, holding it, investing it, and earning compound investment income on it until that dollar is either paid out in the form of a claim or it is redistributed in the form of profits back to the insurance company's shareholders.

At a high level, the captive is all about transferring those two benefits away from insurance companies, to individual companies within the captive.

At the core, a captive insurance company is a risk financing tool. Ultimately, these underwriting profits, as well as the monies that are set aside and invested for reserves, as well as the growth in those funds, are hopefully returned to those captive owners. This feeling is especially true with business owners that manage their risks and their risk profile very well. Those that strive to be safe and have very few claims and injuries, that ultimately pay far, far more in premium than the insurance company pays out in losses. When you have the mindset that you do not want to have injuries or claims, and you get together with other like-minded businesses, you can see that as a group you can insure yourselves at a much more efficient means than the traditional insurance marketplace.

There are also situations where the traditional insurance marketplace will not provide coverage for you for the risks that you face as an organization. In these situations, you are retaining those losses as a company, to retain any losses you have to set aside money. That money you need to set aside ends up being considered profit and is taxable. Insuring risks in a captive can be a legitimate business expense. A captive gives you the ability to customize your coverage, and to provide coverage that you cannot buy in the insurance marketplace. Basically, it gives you flexible coverage and flexible terms.

So, why are the numbers of captives exploding? It is because smaller companies, particularly those that are be paying as low as $100,000 in premium are now eligible to join group captives, and as a result the group captive world has grown to a point that they have become more efficient in handling businesses of this size.

Being a member of a captive is quite interesting in that you get to act as your own insurance company, and also potentially receive the benefits of owning your own insurance company, including underwriting profit and investment income.

The key concept behind captive insurance is, in essence, self-insuring your risks. You do not completely leave the traditional insurance marketplace, because there are still risks that you may choose not to self-insure, and you may still need a licensed insurance company to assist you when a licensed insurance company is required, such as the case with workers' compensation or auto liability insurance. States typically require a licensed insurance company for these types of coverage.

You might think that self-insurance is too much for you. But every business is basically self-insuring; it is just a matter of to what degree. Every business that buys an insurance policy has a retention that they are self-insuring, also known as a deductible.

You may choose a low or a high deductible for retention. Think of it this way: if you were to add or raise your deductible on your general liability insurance from $1,000 to $10,000 and your premium was reduced by $5,000 a year, you may choose to increase your self-insurance amount because you feel that, over time, you are going to reap the rewards of that higher retention by saving premium over time. The concept of a captive just takes it to a higher level.

The concept of using a captive is like taking advantage of using larger deductibles, and captives allow you to control what you will have to ultimately pay for your insurance protection, all while reaping the benefits when you perform better than the worst-case scenario. The advantage of a group captive is that you get to take advantage of those large deductible premium savings without having to face the prospects of paying the entire large deductible yourself; the group in the captive will help you.

Just so you know the same concern over paying out huge claims applies to insurance companies as well. They do not want to take on millions of dollars in claims by themselves, so they go out and buy insurance themselves, which is called reinsurance. They keep only a portion of the potential claims, say the first $250,000 or $500,000 of a claim, and then let the reinsurance take care of the big claims. As the chance of something occurring that will bring about a claim of over $250,000 is very small, the cost of reinsurance is significantly lower as compared to the cost of insurance for the first $250,000.

How money flows in an Insurance Company

"Insurance"   **"Reinsurance"**

| Your Company | Premium Payments → ← Claim Payments | Insurance Company | Excess Coverage Premium Payments → ← Claim Payments | Excess Per Claim & Aggregate Reinsurance Insurance Company |

The insurance companies can charge the largest amount of their premiums, and make most of their profits, from insuring these small, predictable claims and letting others (reinsurance companies) take on the large, unpredictable million dollar claims.

From the "insurance side," a captive insurance program looks, acts and feels like a typical guaranteed cost insurance program. You purchase a standard, guaranteed cost insurance policy from and pay premiums to a regulated insurance company. The insurance company, or an approved Third Party Administrator, will pay your claims. You will be able to deduct your premium when it comes to taxes, and you will even have a year-end premium audit. No one outside of your company will know that you are an owner of a captive or that your policies are reinsured by your captive.

On the "captive side" is where things change.

Your captive enables you, individually or as part of a group, to fund and pay for those smaller, predictable claims. Therefore, the potential underwriting and investment income profits, which normally would go to the insurance company to insure poorer quality businesses and benefit their shareholders, would go to you or the group. In essence, you are able to bypass the insurance company in the traditional insurance model and access the reinsurance marketplace directly to take care of those large, unpredictable claims, thereby dramatically reducing your insurance costs.

As a captive cannot issue policies directly to the general public, and because coverages like workers' compensation and auto liability statutorily require a licensed insurance company, a captive uses a licensed "fronting" insurance company to issue the policies for the captive. The fronting company keeps a small percentage fee for the issuance of your insurance policies and dealing with any necessary regulations, state or federal filings, etc. The fronting company will then "buy" reinsurance from your captive and send it the net remaining premium. The fronting company is just what its name implies; it is the front or outward face of your insurance program.

How money flows in Captive Insurance Companies

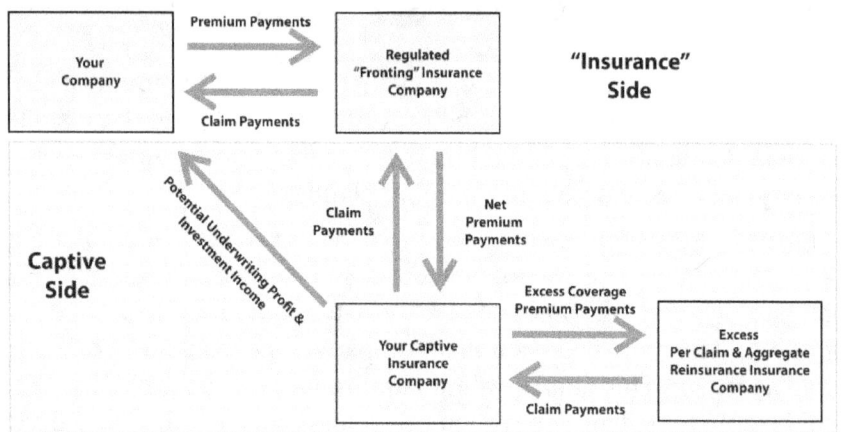

As you can now see, your captive insurance company will really be a reinsurance company for your policies. Instead of insuring the large, unpredictable claims, you or your group insure the smaller, predictable ones and then buy your own reinsurance for the large, unpredictable claims.

Your captive insurance company will manage and pay all of the claims for you or your group. After all expenses and amounts are paid out for claims, and if your captive takes in more money than it spends, it generates an underwriting profit that may be returned to you as the owner(s) of the captive.

However, much like a regular insurance company, you do not want to have your captive pay for all of your potential claims by itself. Therefore, you must purchase reinsurance for the captive in order to limit what you may have to potentially pay out. Through the reinsurance your captive purchases, your captive insurance company will function much like a high-deductible program. The captive will pay for claims up to an amount where any single claim (see A in Captive Program diagram below) or all claims in aggregate (see C in Captive Program diagram below) exceed a certain threshold where your reinsurance (your captive purchases from another insurance company) starts to provide excess coverage.

After one or both of these deductibles have been exceeded, the excess reinsurance that the captive purchased will pay any additional claim amounts. The excess reinsurance thereby limits how much you may have to pay out for claims in a particular year.

Captive Program Diagram

Whereas the captive is an insurance company that has to pay the operating expenses, in addition to paying a premium to fund your claims you will need to pay fees for the fronting insurance company, the captive's reinsurance company, the third-party claims administrator, and other normal operating costs of an insurance company.

However, just as with traditional insurance companies, the premiums that are received by your captive are not spent right away. They need to be set aside as reserves to pay claims. While the monies are held by the captive, the funds can be invested and any proceeds are available to pay claims or be returned as profits to the captive owners. Therefore, you may receive investment income to help pay for your claims and/or be returned to you as part of the captive's profits.

The standard insurance market is based on the law of large numbers. Better run businesses with fewer claims subsidize those with more claims. Those "better" businesses, that are well-run and safety-focused, can qualify to come out of the standard market and insure themselves in a captive program where the collective risk is significantly lower than in the general insurance pool. Since these businesses will have fewer claims, they will earn lower premiums than they would in the traditional market. Over time, most members earn very significant premium reductions.

Your premiums are determined by actuaries based solely on your individual claims history, not by general industry averages or insurance companies. Remember, captive members typically have better claims histories than the industry average and therefore having premiums based solely on their history will result in lower costs. Since members in a captive typically improve their claims performance year after year, this compounding of lower claims every year can produce rates for you that are dramatically lower than the industry average.

Approximately 40% of your premiums will be used to cover the expenses of your captive program. This will include the fronting company fee, the reinsurance for your captive, the claims management costs, agent commission, as well as other captive operating costs.

This lower cost structure of a captive allows approximately 60% of your premium to be seeded into your Initial Loss Fund (see B in Captive Program diagram below), as shown in the diagram above. If you do not completely use your Loss Fund, it will remain in your "account" for later distribution, potentially earning investment income. Also, since those claims that do occur are not paid immediately, the required claim reserves will also be set aside and invested with any investment proceeds also going to your account. As you can see, investment income is a significant way to help pay for potential claims as well as something to be returned to you later as a dividend.

However, as there is the possibility that your actual losses may exceed the amount estimated for your Loss Fund, you must also set aside additional funds or a letter of credit to guarantee payment for the Potential Loss Fund Gap (see B– C in Captive Program diagram above), also shown in the diagram above. The Potential Loss Fund Gap is the total amount you may have to pay if all of your losses exceed the Initial Loss Fund, and before remaining claims costs are picked up by the reinsurance company.

If all goes well and you have fewer if any claims, you will reap the rewards of both underwriting and investment profit via dividends. However, you do have the potential to pay additional funds when you have a bad year. In the group captive world, if the entire group has a bad year, which is extremely rare, you may need to pay into that Potential Loss Fund Gap as well.

It is important to remember that you have a per claim reinsurance program, and therefore a single catastrophic claim would not cause a member or all members to be affected as there is still a per claim threshold in which that catastrophic claim would then be transferred to the reinsurance company. It is a myth that a single claim can bring a captive down. The only reason the Potential Loss Fund Gap would need to be funded would be if there were an unexpected, very significant frequency of claims. With a member or group of members being so focused on safety and claims management, the likelihood of a frequency problem to arise would also be rare.

There are many advantages to a captive, two of which are the dividend of the underwriting profit and any investment income, and premium deductibility for tax purposes including the amount paid in for your loss funds. The dividend that you may earn will typically be significantly larger than what you could have received with a dividend plan as those typically stop if your loss ratio is over 25%, 30% or 35%. With 60% of your premium being used to cover claims, it provides you with a potential 35%, 30% or 25% return of underwriting profits respectfully, plus any investment income. Your potential "profits" will be returned as a dividend, and may be taxed as capital gains depending upon your captive ownership structure and nature, should your captive declare a dividend several years down the road. With an 831(b) captive, the dividends are typically received as a capital gain. However, captives insuring workers' compensation and general and auto liability are typically treated as ordinary income. It is best to discuss with the captive manager and your accountant as to how dividends would be treated based on the type and ownership structure of the captive.

In comparison, with high-deductible and self-insurance, only paid claims can be deducted for tax purposes, and you will have to pay taxes on the claim reserves you set aside. Your captive's board will determine the amount of any dividends and when they will be paid. However, all accrued funds are eventually returned to you.

When it comes to distributing any underwriting profits and investment income, similar to a retrospectively-rated or high-deductible program, the period at which your captive adjusts the losses could take three to five years to play out and for the captive year to close. It takes a long-term investment for the dividend to be paid. But clearly it is not going to return the profits of the captive as quickly as a dividend program. We will go through how a captive closes claims and distributes potential profits in Chapter 7.

As you can see, the combination of shrinking premiums and the return of underwriting profits to you translate into an overall dramatically reduced cost to insure a business as compared to the traditional insurance marketplace.

Still, businesses in a captive typically also receive the additional benefit from **Greater Control over their Risk Management Program** due to an excessive pricing, limited capacity, coverage that are unavailable in the "traditional" insurance market, and/or the desire for a more cost-efficient risk financing mechanism. They are able to achieve that control through **improved cash-flow, transparency, the ability to customize coverage, improve claims handling and reporting**, and **stabilized budgets**.

Improved Claims Handling and Reporting

I have heard business leaders complain that there is an injured employee that they know should be working. They have either seen the employee doing something that they medically should not be doing, or maybe working for someone else under the table. In the traditional insurance world, the insurance company is in control of what happens. They may believe that ordering surveillance can be a costly long-shot, or that an IME (Independent Medical Evaluation) may be too costly versus what they believe the possibility of success to be. However, in the captive world, as you are paying those claim costs yourself, you can control having someone investigated.

The insurance industry is set up to handle the mass quantity of small claims like broken windshields, small fender benders, and medical only injuries. The problem is that those claims distract the adjusters from handling the larger, more complex claims that could cost you significant dollars. This could lead to smaller injuries becoming costly ones, which can cost you money. The captive programs address this issue head on.

As you can see, captive insurance provides member businesses much greater control over their claims management. If a captive member is concerned about the legitimacy of a claim, they can call for an investigation. Conversely, if they would like it closed and settled quickly, that is what occurs. With advice from the Captive Management Company, the third-party administrator, the member's attorney and insurance broker, the captive member makes the decisions that they believe are in their best interest.

Ability to Custom Tailor Coverage

The standard general liability policy has exclusion for "your product." Therefore, insurance companies do not pay for damages to your product, only for the resulting bodily injury or property damage. Therefore, a manufacturer of food products runs the risk that their food could become contaminated, but the contamination is not revealed before it is shipped to consumers. A standard general liability policy does not cover the cost of recalling their product, the cost to advertise to the public, or to send communication directly to consumers to alert them of the issue. Nor does it cover the cost of replacing the food item, the cost of disposing of the bad food, and the cost of hiring a public relations firm to help maintain or restore the image of the manufacturer in the public's eye. In a captive, you can either add coverage for such an issue, or simply remove the exclusion, because you can control the coverage.

Many captives are established because insurance in the commercial insurance market is prohibitively expensive, poorly matched to the business' needs, or not available at all. A captive insurance company can successfully provide coverage for difficult risks that are tailored to fit the exact needs of the business – as long as the captive operates within sound underwriting, actuarial, and regulatory guidelines.

Stability in Pricing and Availability

Pricing stability is achieved over time as a captive matures and expands its own risk retention capability. The more capital that is accumulated, the greater the captive insurance company's ability to retain risk and insulate itself from changes in the commercial insurance market. A captive can also provide stability in the availability of coverage.

Transparency

Since you are an owner of the captive insurance company, there is complete transparency. You will know how every dollar of your premium is being used, and in a group captive, how every other member's premiums are used as well. You will have access to all captive's financial information. You can see how much is spent to pay claims, to issue policies, provide claims management and loss control services, to secure reinsurance and cover general overhead.

Improved Cash Flow (Return of Unused Premiums)

Cash flow improvements are achieved in a number of ways. The premiums you pay to cover losses and potential losses are normal business expenses ("tax deductible"), as are monies set aside for claim reserves and things such as Incurred But Not Reported claims. If these losses are retained yourself ("self-insured"), a business would have to pay taxes on those funds they have to set aside.

When an insurance company uses less money to pay claims than it takes in, the unused monies generate an underwriting profit for the insurance company. In the captive world, the underwriting profits, and gains from the invested premiums, that would otherwise be held by a conventional insurance company are retained by the captive. Even with conservative investment portfolios, the dollar amounts are substantial due to the high levels of capital and surplus typically held.

The proceeds are eventually returned to the captive owners rather than to the shareholders of a traditional insurance company.

This ability to return underwriting profits to you will also provide the incentive and the financial reward to increase your focus even more on preventing and reducing injuries and claims.

Finally, cash flow is improved by reducing the expense factors associated with commercial insurance. Generally, insurance companies allocate 50-55% of premiums they receive to loss payments, while the other 45-50% covers expenses and profits. Captives have far fewer expense components than do commercial insurance companies. Estimates for the expense components of captives typically fall in the 30-40% range. This means that for every $10 million in net written premium, a successful operating captive can save business owners $1 million to $2.5 million in expenses alone. Successful group captives allow their members to also share proportionally in these savings.

Increased Control over the Program

Ownership and control by its owners distinguish a captive insurer from a commercial insurance company. This is not the type of ownership or control evidenced by a nominal percentage share in the company's surplus. It means ownership in the company's strategic business purpose.

Captive insurers offer increased control in a number of other ways as well. For one, captive owners have more control over insurance-related services such as safety and loss control, as well as claims administration. Safety and loss control services established by a captive can be tailored to each participant's individual needs, resulting in safer workplaces and more favorable loss experience. Claims handling services are unbundled and arranged separately. Strict guidelines can be drafted and enforced by the captive. This is preferable to allowing a commercial insurance company, whose interests might be more self-serving, to dictate how claims are handled.

What is a Captive?

Types of Captives

To better grasp the benefits of captive insurance, it is important to understand that there are a variety of types of captives developed to deliver specific benefits to specific business types.

There are several types of captives: Single Parent (Pure), Group, Association, Agency and 831(b)(Enterprise).

Single Parent Captive (Pure Captive)

If you are paying a significant amount in premium, typically a million dollars or more in casualty premiums, you may want to form your own captive so you are not sharing risks with other companies not related to you. The single parent captive is a legal entity formed separately as a subsidiary to a parent organization. The parent controls the captive to insure the parent company and its affiliates. It gives the parent company the ability to directly access the reinsurance market, as well as customize your insurance program, thereby reducing the costs of protecting your business while improving your insurance program.

Group Captive

A Group Captive entails joining with a group of other companies that also have a significant focus on preventing and mitigating claims. In a group captive, you may be able to enter the captive for as little as $75,000 of casualty premiums. Casualty premiums are premiums for your "liability" coverage, such as workers' compensation, general liability, and auto coverage. However, some group captives require $250,000 or more for casualty lines premium. Due to the lower premium requirement as an entry point, as compared to self-insurance, you can receive a significantly lower Total Cost of Risk that is similar to that of self-insurance, plus you do not have to deal with all the regulatory headaches associated with being self-insured. In addition, participating in a captive can have tax advantages over self-insurance as well. Because of these advantages, you can see why Group Captives are the most popular form of alternative risk financing.

Association Captive

In some situations, an association may form a group captive to benefit the members of the association or a specific industry. In those circumstances it is not uncommon for the association program to include coverage needed by the members that may not be available in the marketplace, or would require them to purchase multiple separate policies.

Agency Captive

Sometimes, an insurance agency or broker may form a captive insurance company to underwrite and insure (or reinsure) a number of their business clients. The agent may do that because they believe their clients' policies will produce an underwriting profit and the agency is looking to expand its sources of revenue. It also allows the ability to offer a more competitive program, either via specialty coverage or rates.

831(b) Captive (Micro or Enterprise Risk Captive)

The Tax Reform Act of 1986 created the 831(b) section of the Internal Revenue Code, making it advantageous for small and mid-market companies to own their own insurance company. Therefore, 831(b) is really a tax election that allows small captives with gross premium income of less than $2.2 million annually to pay taxes solely on investment income and not on any underwriting profit. It may also allow for the tax deductibility of premiums, as well as the proceeds/dividends of captives being taxed as a capital gain in lieu of ordinary income depending upon the captive's ownership should the captive meet the risk sharing and distribution requirements laid out in the IRS code. These are often called "micro-captives." There is more on 831(b) Enterprise Captives in Chapter 8.

Structures of Captives

When dealing with a traditional captive versus rent-a-captives or multi-cell captives, there are several structures you could be involved in:

- **Single Cell Captive.** There is only one organization in the legally filed captive company. A single cell captive can be formed to benefit a single company (Single Parent) or multiple companies (Group, Association, or Agency).

- **Multi-Cell (Rent-A-Captive).** These are captives structured so there is one large captive company that allows multiple captives to be formed and operate inside of it. Think of these multi-cell captives as being similar to a condominium building. You have your own unit, but you are one of many units in the condominium building. Multi-Cell Captives allows businesses or groups to enter into a captive program more economically as they will not have all the frictional costs of setting up their own captive.

  - **Traditional Multi-Cell Captive.** Each of the captives in the large captive insures the risks of those separate captives whether they are a single parent, group, association, agency, etc. However, if one of the captive cells undergoes significant financial problems there may be collateral damage to the other cells in the captive, much like a fire in one condominium unit may cause collateral damage to surrounding units.

  - **Segregated (Protected) Cell Multi-Cell Captive.** Similar to that of a Multi-Cell or Rent-A-Captive in that there are multiple captives formed within the larger captive structure. However, there is a regulatory barrier between cells that protects each cell from each other. It is like having a super-firewall existing between each condominium unit. No damage is going to occur outside that segregated cell. Therefore, you do not need to worry about the risk resulting from another captive cell collapsing.

Types of Captives

Choosing a Captive Domiciles

Captive insurance companies must be formed, located, licensed, filed to do business and approved by a governmental body, which is referred to as their place of domicile. When you establish a captive, it needs to follow the rules and regulations of the domicile. There are over 100 domiciles in the world, so it is important that you choose the place that best suits you.

Most captives are legally created outside the United States, but those inside of the United States are growing as states improve their rules and regulations in order to establish captives within their state borders, making them more attractive as an option to foreign domiciles.

At the time of writing this, the **top 20 domiciles** for captives were:

Bermuda

Cayman Islands

Vermont

Guernsey

Luxembourg

Barbados

Delaware

Ireland

British Virgin Islands

Hawaii

South Carolina

Isle of Man

Nevada

Arizona

Utah

Turks & Caicos

Singapore

Sweden

Switzerland

District of Columbia

The use of multi-cell captives has grown because it is more cost effective to rent a cell rather than to build your own captive. If you explore your own captive, or participate in a group captive, it is important to work with your captive manager to understand the structure of the captive you will participate in. By doing so you will confirm that the jurisdiction you choose for the captive has the ability for segregated cell captives to better protect your overall investment.

What to look for in choosing a domicile:

- Political stability
- Regulations
- Coverage Allowed
- Ease of Access
- Support Service Availability
- Cost

Political Stability

We are not worried about a political coupe in Vermont. When we look at political stability, we are looking at the legislative and judicial support of captives. In other words, if Democrats support captives and the Republicans win the election, there may be change in support of captives for the better or for the worse.

Same applies to offshore domiciles too. The Bahamas were once a significant destination of captives. At one point, the leadership of the government changed and due to new laws, the captives left. Think of it this way, if the new governor or leader of a country is looking for revenue and decides that imposing significant taxes on captives is a good thing, the captives will leave to find another favorable domicile.

Regulations

Solid regulations are important for two reasons. First, if there is no government oversight, or incompetent oversight, and a captive can do what they want, then a fronting insurance company will be uncomfortable in being property protected when it comes to being reinsured for losses that are being paid. Second, if the amount of oversight is so onerous, problematic and costly to do business in that domicile, then no captive manager would want to set up and manage a captive in that domicile. As you can see, a balance is needed.

Coverage Allowed

You must be absolutely certain about the state or country in which your captive is domiciled and that what you propose to insure through it is legal. For example, placing workers' compensation in a captive domiciled in Arizona is very difficult as doing so would also have to fulfill the regulations of meeting the self-insured requirements of that state's insurance department.

Another example is punitive damages. Whereas insuring it is generally against public policy inside the United States, it is allowable to do so in most foreign domiciles. Placing warranty coverage inside a domestic captive is also a challenge as it is typically not viewed as insurance; therefore, the programs that provide warranty coverage in a captive for United Stated retailers and auto dealerships are generally domiciled offshore.

Ease of Access

Although you might be thinking the importance of access is that of access to captive support systems and financial institutions, that is actually next up in supportive services. When it comes to access, we are talking about how you access the domicile itself, in other words, we are looking at how you physically get to the domicile. Most captive domiciles require a meeting to occur in the domicile, therefore the logistics are important, such as is it easy to get there, are there frequent flights, are accommodations nice and available, is traveling there reasonable in terms of cost?

Jetting off to a Caribbean island certainly sounds nice, but in today's hectic world having to take a whole day to get to a two or three-day meeting and another whole day to return may be a bit much. Some require annual meetings to be in the domicile and others may only require you to return to the domicile once every three years. Therefore, ease of travel and time to travel is important, however, going to a destination that you enjoy is certainly a plus.

You will note that any foreign based domicile captive will lead to all business meetings occurring outside of the United States.

Support Service Availability

Now that you have arrived and enjoyed the attractions the captive domicile provides, it is time to roll up your sleeves and do a little bit of work. To run a captive, your domicile needs to have all of the support services available that you need, such as several domicile captive managers that you can choose from, typically a strong actuary, an attorney, a banker, and even an accountant. If these are not present at your place of domicile, the complexity of running a captive becomes greater.

Your domicile captive manager provides the day-to-day captive management, acts as your liaison between the captive and local regulators, keeps the books, reviews the contracts, etc. They will also need to be located in your domicile and be in good standing with the local government regulators.

Cost

Capitalization of the captive will most likely be a significant cost. The amount of collateral needed will vary by domicile, and I have seen them vary from $100,000 to over $1,000,000. Although the collateral may be returned should you close the captive, that collateral is tied up for as long as you are participating in the captive.

In addition to the collateral, there will be annual fees, cost of actuarial and regulatory reviews or audits, and annual meeting costs. You will also need to pay for your costs to travel to the meeting.

If your captive is offshore, there is also the Federal Excise Tax that would need to be paid as the premiums would leave the United States.

It is important to look at all of the costs as part of the decision in choosing a domicile. Yes, a trip to beautiful beaches and great scuba diving reefs of the Grand Caymans is always fun, but the favorable political climate and regulations, availability of support services, and ease of traveling inside the United States (as well as generally being free of snow year rounds is a big plus) is allowing South Carolina to quickly climb the ladder of domicile locations.

Joining a Captive

Is Joining a Group Captive Right for Me?

Generally speaking, it is easy to determine if you might be a good fit for a captive. You just ask yourself the following questions:

- Do I have a strong focus on employee safety and a great corporate culture?
- Am I a privately-held mid-market company with predictable risks?
- Do I pay over a $100,000 annually in workers' compensation, general liability and auto insurance combined premiums, or insure over 20 employees on my health insurance program?
- If I review my last five to 10 years of claims history, on average, are my total claims paid out less than 40% of the total premium paid to insurance companies over a period of several years? (For this calculation, cap any claim over $100,000 at $100,000 when you calculate your claims to premiums ratio.)
- Is my business financially strong with a positive cash flow?

If you can answer YES to these questions, a group captive may make financial sense. It is important to know that every captive member will need to be able to meet their claims obligations, and therefore they are financially reviewed by the captive manager. Because of this, each member business puts up collateral (or posts a letter of credit) in the first few years until their asset account has accumulated to a sufficient level.

There are additional nuances that help determine how much a business will benefit from joining a group captive. A broker with experience in group captive insurance programs will do a more complete evaluation once a business is identified as a likely candidate.

As the success of your participation in a captive is ultimately linked to your success in managing your claims or losses, your focus on managing and controlling your risks, your claims, and focusing on safety and preventing injuries and claims from occurring is vital. Therefore, the following chapters in this book will be critical to your success:

- Benchmarking
- Improving Safety and Utilizing Behavior Based Safety/ Employee Management
- Understanding Effective Risk Management
- Managing Claims
- Improved Hiring for Selecting Better Performing Employees
- Choosing the Right Broker to Help You Look at Captives
- These are the items needed to be added to the book, are there any other items of concepts that need to be added here?

How do I Join a Group Captive?

When considering making a move to a group captive insurance program, the decision-making process is different than renewing your business insurance in the traditional market, where price and service level are generally the driving factors. This is because a group captive program is a different method of purchasing insurance as it also establishes a separate mechanism for growing and preserving financial assets outside of your existing business.

In addition to looking at the premium and claims payment history of a business, the captive manager will look at a number of other operational factors, including:

- Length of ownership
  - o Captives normally will want a business that has been functional for five years

- o However, if the past experience in operations is there, they may allow only three years in business.
- Financial strength
  - o As you are responsible for paying your claims, the captive will need to make sure you are financially sound and capable of paying them so that they can protect the other members in your captive as well as the fronting and reinsurance companies.
- North American Industry Classification System (NAICS) Code
  - o They will look at what industry you are in and determine if you meet the guidelines of the fronting and reinsurance companies.

The full analysis and qualification process can take two to six months. For this reason, it is not recommended that the evaluation of a group captive program be conducted in conjunction with a business' regular annual insurance renewal.

When determining the value and projected annual premium with a group captive program, it is important to understand that conventional bidding and negotiation of rates is not part of the process. Captives do not use the rates filed with regulatory agencies, but rather establish premiums, that are developed by an actuary using various calculation methods in determining your loss fund, sometimes referred to as a "loss pick". These determinations use five years of claims and premium data to determine the premium amount and claims fund deposit needed to protect the other members of the captive.

These actuarial forecasts tend to be conservative (more expensive) in the early years of captive membership because, as most business owners are aware, captives have differing claims reserves and payment practices. As a business ages in a captive program, the claims experience becomes more predictable because the claims reserving and payment strategy is set by the captive owners. This results in more significant cost savings and asset growth over time. (We will be going more in-depth into the actuarial review in the next chapter.)

The process of joining a captive will take between three weeks to three months depending on the complexity of the business considering the option and the workload of the captive management company.

	Action Step	Duration	By Whom
1	Collect 5 years of claims and premium history	1-2 weeks	Business owner
2	Prepare pro-forma	2 days	Insurance broker
3	Submit to the captive for actuarial review and approval	2 weeks – 2 months	
4	Review captive memorandum and other documents	1-2 days	Business owner
5	Review the captive cost and premium calculation - *Captive financials should be reviewed at this time*	2 hours	Presentation typically done by the broker and captive manager
6	Purchase captive stock and make the first captive premium payment	Upon inception of the insurance coverage	
7	Post collateral in either cash or a letter of credit	Up to 30 days following the inception of coverage	

Captive Actuarial Review

The captive actuarial review, or feasibility study, is the most important part of the process in looking at the possibility of starting or joining a captive. It is also the biggest area of "mystery" for business owners when contemplating the purpose of establishing or entering the captive is feasible. It also decides how a captive determines the amount that a business owner entering a captive will need to set aside for potential claims and pay out for captive operational expenses. In other words, what will the premium be?

Every business owner must do a cost benefit analysis when determining if joining a captive makes sense for them. Not doing so would be foolhardy.

Business owners will typically look at their own claims history and determine if the financial/premium model laid out by the captive would have generated the business owner underwriting and investment income for a period of the last five to 10 years. Over a 10-year period, a business will possibly experience a bad year only once, where they will have an extremely large, unexpected claim in addition to other claims. In another year or two they may have several more claims, but nothing extreme. But most likely, in seven or eight of those years, not much happens at all. In this case, the business owner will reap the significant rewards of the underwriting profits and investment income in seven or eight of those 10 years. They will have one or two years where they will likely receive a minor return of underwriting profit and investment income, and possibly that one bad year, with that huge claim as well as others, will cause them to have to pay in additional funds (with a known maximum amount) to cover their claims. When the business owner believes that over those 10 years they will financially benefit from a captive, it makes sense to join.

The captive does a similar analysis to determine if having that business be in a captive makes financial sense. In order to do that, the captive must determine what the predicted loss fund and expense amounts would need to be. Even though a captive is a type of insurance company, it is not a *traditional* insurance company which files rates. A captive cannot turn to a manual and see that they should charge $1,643 for a 2015 Ford F450 Pickup with $1,000,000 liability coverage and $500 comprehensive and collision deductibles. Therefore, the captive turns to actuaries to determine that.

Being a graduate from Penn State University's Risk Management and Insurance department, I have several friends that are actuaries. Actuaries are mathematically-inclined business professionals who deal with the measurement and management of risk and uncertainty. Actuaries provide assessments of financial security systems, with a focus on their complexity, their mathematics, and their mechanisms. In English, they calculate probabilities that losses or claims will occur.

Actuaries require enough data to get a credible loss funding amount, but do not want to use data that was around from the Reagan administration. They want to keep the data current enough to reflect current conditions as they are going to have to benchmark loss ratios, loss development patterns and trend factors based on broad industry data sources. Since insurance data is expensive, the best granular insurance data is going to be data that they collect on the captive program itself. For example, as a captive matures they can gather data and determine the nature of the risk's operations and identify the projected exposure.

When it comes to workers' compensation, one of the biggest drivers of expected losses is going to be where the business is located. California businesses will behave differently than, say, Illinois businesses. For general liability, there is going to be a difference between a risk for a chain of dollar stores as compared to a business that manufactures chainsaws. Actuaries would use different assumptions for the general liability as well. As you can see, there are a lot of variables that an actuary will need to look at when determining the predicted loss funding.

Unlike traditional insurance companies, captives do not have specific rates they charge. They will determine your loss fund and premium using your own historical data. For each coverage you look to place into a captive, such as workers' compensation, auto liability or general liability, the actuaries will need to receive your historical claims data in terms of amounts, both paid and reserved, for your total incurred amounts for five years. They will also need to trend these based upon the fluctuations that occur within your business: i.e. how much your revenues have increased or decreased each year for your general liability exposure, how many vehicles did you have for your auto liability, and how much payroll did you have each year for your workers' compensation coverage.

They will also need your prior premiums by year for each of the coverages they are conducting their actuarial analysis for. When it comes to required data, the number one question I receive from business owners is, "Why do they need my premiums?". Upon deeper discussion the business owners have asserted that this concern stems from when they received insurance quotes in the past that the quotes seemed to come in only a little under their expiring premiums, and because of this they do not like to provide information on their premiums. In a traditional insurance world, I understand their concerns. However, in the captive world, as you will see, it is not something to be worried about.

But here is why premiums are actuarially required. No one would second guess the actuary's use of your past claims history to determine what your future probable claims are. Thus, there are three problems with using *only* your data:

1. You are only one company and are not actuarily large enough to be independent. Yes, your specific history may be indicative of what your future claims *may* look like, but actuarially speaking, your possible claims in the future will certainly not be identical. You may experience changes based on what is occurring in your industry or legal environment, plus you could still have possibly one huge, unexpected claim that your historical data did not show in the past.

2. There is the zero ($0) affect. For example, perhaps you have gone years without a general liability claim, or maybe never had one. Does this guarantee that you will *never* have one? Of course not. Mathematically, anything times zero, is still zero.

If your historical data has no claims, how can the captive collect a reasonable premium to pay for potential claims? Does it seem fair that someone that had no general liability claims for five years used this information in their premium calculation period, and therefore were not charged a premium for the coverage, but yet still have that unexpected claim paid by the group?

3. The issue of time and reality. When the actuary looks at data, they can only look at what occurred during that specific time frame. They cannot see that there is a lawsuit or claim that has already happened, but has not been reported to the insurance company and therefore not on your loss runs. This is an actuarial certainty, and the industry has a term for it known as IBNR -Incurred But Not Reported. Actuaries must take IBNR into account. Face it, someone may fall today but not report their injury to you for a week or a month, but still slip the lawsuit in just under the statute of limitation wire. You cannot report something you do not know. The insurance company cannot adjust nor reserve for a claim they do not know about, but the actuaries can add IBNR to the overall claim to allow for that inevitable claim to be found out about later. Accounting for and reserving for IBNR is statutorily required so that insurance companies have monies set aside to pay for future potential claims.

To expand further, many actuaries use the Bornhuetter-Ferguson method to estimate the incurred but not yet reported (IBNR) losses for a policy year. This technique was created by two actuaries, Bornhuetter and Ferguson, and was first introduced to the actuary world back in 1975. Many actuaries use it today as it combines features of the Chain Ladder Method and the Expected Loss Ratio Method.

The Chain Ladder Method calculates IBNR by examining the point over a period in time, usually greater than 10 years, in which a claim is reported and eventually paid. They create historical loss triangles so that they can estimate IBNR for future possible claims.

The Expected Loss Ratio (ELR) Method is the main reason that the captive actuaries *require* your historical premiums. ELR is a technique used to determine the projected amount of claims relative to your historical premiums the insurance companies collected. Actuaries use ELR because they do not have filed rates and using only your data lacks a large enough sample for long-tail coverage lines such as workers' compensation, general liability and auto liability.

As captives do not have rates, they will assume that a portion of your historical premium has been set aside by the insurance company in order to pay for future claims. A traditional insurance company will determine potential claims depending on the frequency and severity they expect to experience, and use those forecasts to calculate their final rates they will use for premium calculations by adding in expense costs. In other words, ELR does reverse engineering to determine what the traditional insurance company expected to use in terms of claim costs based on your premiums.

For example, a business paid a premium of $500,000 for their workers' compensation coverage in 2016. Let us also assume that the expected loss ratio was 60%, or 0.60. During the 2016 policy, they paid $100,000 in claims for the year. The insurance company was expecting 60% or $300,000 ($500,000 x 0.60) and therefore would still need to statutorily reserve $200,000 ($300,000 expected - $100,000 paid) for IBNR. In this example, using ELR, the captive actuary would use the $300,000 as the expected losses for that policy year. Blending five years of historical ELR, along with the businesses' historical claims data for those years, the actuary will determine the loss fund to be used in their upcoming policy year.

As you can see, an actuary uses a combination of methods including your historical data and what would be expected based on your historical premium in order to determine what your loss fund should be. The important thing to remember is that even if you feel that the loss fund is higher than you think it should be, that excess is underwriting profit that will be returned to you. Plus, the premiums and reserves do not just sit there; they are working for you by earning investment income.

Once you understand this key concept, you will then be able to understand why we have routinely seen businesses enter into captives. It's because they actually pay more initial premium to their captive program than they would to a traditional insurance program. As a result, they would receive their underwriting profit back from their captive and none from a traditional insurance company. Plus, they would also lose all of the other captive benefits if they stayed in a traditional insurance program.

I would also think you would want a more accurate representation of your potential claims and an appropriate loss fund rather than a "more attractive premium" from an underestimated loss fund that could lead to paying more in to cover your claims.

––––––––––––

Captive Profit Distributions

After your captive year, you will be reviewing your captive's financial statement, staring at any underwriting profits and investment income that your loss fund and the captive accumulated. While you are thinking of what can you do with the money, it is important to know that you cannot just grab the money and run. You need to wait for claims to be reported and paid, so let us run through what your financial statement might look like.

Whether you are in a single parent captive, or in a group captive, the financial statements will be similar in structure. Much like a business Income & Expense Statement, you will see Income (Premium & Investment Income), Expenses (Operating and Claims), and ultimately Profit/Loss (Equity). We will break this down in detail later.

There are variations when it comes to a group captive, as how the captive is structured will make a difference. With group captives, there are two common structures for the loss fund: Individual Accounts or Shared Account.

Individual Accounts

Group Captives with Individual Accounts you will have the separate financials showing each member's financial statement separately. It will show when risk sharing occurs and the amount of risk sharing assigned to each member. In the end, each member will know what their own individual results will be.

For privacy purposes, typically captive owner names are not identified on the reports, they are identified by numbers. You will only know your number, and as some group captives have hundreds of members, you will have some privacy then.

Any member can have a bad year, that is why you buy insurance. However, when a member has multiple, four or five, years in a row of poor performance, the group may ask that member to leave. However, when the group needs to make that kind of decision relating to a member that has had multiple years of poor performance, the member's name is not known. This way the group is making a business decision and not a personal one.

This structure is the most common with workers' compensation and liability group captives.

Shared Account

With a Shared Account structure, there is no individual financial statement. The group will share the underwriting profit, or loss, and investment income. Dividend distribution is based on a percentage of premium paid into the captive. In other words, the largest premium paying company receives the largest dividend; the smallest receives the smallest. Everything is in proportion.

The captive manager typically has loss and premium information separated by each business. This way any member with continuous poor performance can be identified and the captive board, or members, can vote on what to do. The loss performance of the individual member may or may not be shared with the members, the captive manager may just generically deliver the member's results, or when details are shared, usually only an account number is known. Once again, this way the group is making a business decision and not a personal one.

This structure is the most common with Association Captives as well as Healthcare Captives.

Below is an example of a financial statement from a Group Captive with Individual Accounts:

Sample Captive Financial Statement

2016-2017 Underwriting Year	Member 12345	Member 23456	Member 34567
Gross Premium	123,789	458,745	645,748
Captive Operating Costs	49,516	183,498	258,299
Loss Fund (Net Premium)	74,273	275,247	387,449
Losses Paid	2,457	157,875	124,725
Loss Reserves	3,873	125,000	125,000
Profit (or Loss)	**67,943**	**(7,628)**	**137,724**
Loss Assessment	0	0	0
Loss Sharing (Deficit Allocation)	(69)	7,628	(401)
Final Fund Balance	**67,874**	**0**	**137,323**
Investment Income	**3,587**	**6,250**	**13,116**
Equity Balance	**71,462**	**6,250**	**150,439**

As you can see, each member has their own individual account. You will see each member's annual audited year end premium. From the premium, the captive operating costs are removed: insurance company fronting fee, reinsurance coverage, captive operating expenses, captive manager fee, broker commission, etc. The balance becomes your loss fund.

From the loss fund, the member's claims paid and claim reserves are deducted to calculate the underwriting profit for the member. The Third Party or Insurance Company Adjuster will adjust the loss reserves based on if, or when, those funds are paid out and what is transpiring with the claim (is it getting better or worse from a predicted outcome standpoint). The reserves will be in the investment account and will continue to accumulate any investment income.

Based on your captive rules, should you have a "bad year", there may be a point in which you may have to pay addition funds in due to your individual losses. Typically, we see this when a member has a significant frequency of claims. Anyone can have a single, unexpected claim, and the group will help you out, but when you do not control your claims, you may have to pay in extra if you have too many claims.

You will note in this example, Member 23456 did have that large unexpected claim. Because the member had a claim that exceeded their individual claim retention, the group kicked in to help pay a portion of that claim. That is called Risk Sharing. If there was no risk sharing in a captive, the IRS would view it as self-insurance which would affect the deductibility of your premium. So in this example, you will see in the loss sharing, the other members with available loss funds balances had to kick in and help pay some of the large claim member 23456 had. They each paid in an amount based on a percentage of gross premium they paid.

The Final Fund Balance is in essence their Underwriting Profit for the year.

While monies sit in the member's loss fund, or in reserves, it will potentially earn investment income. Investment income, in addition to improving the member's equity balance, can be used to help a member pay a Loss Assessment should that occur.

Ultimately, at the bottom of the financial statement, you will see the member's Equity Balance.

If this was a Single Parent Captive, you would not see Loss Sharing as there would not be any other member to share a loss with.

Even though the captive underwriting year is over, you still see loss reserves that need to work their way through the process of closing or settling. We also do not see any IBNR – Incurred But Not Reported. Therefore, you cannot declare a dividend, and take your equity and run...

First off, remember, your captive's board will determine the amount of any dividends and when they will be paid, however, all accrued funds are eventually returned to you. They must act in the best interest of the captive and make sure that future liabilities (claims) are able to be paid. So, let us walk through that process.

A captive, just like a traditional insurance company will need to wait to see how things play out so that the captives obligations are taken care of. Claims may take a year or more to close, and they may close for more or less than initially reserved.

Each captive year stands alone. A captive cannot directly pull money from one year to pay for a different year. However, an individual member can take the proceeds from a declared dividend to pay for a loss assessment of another year, but the member cannot take money from their equity to do so.

As things take time, we usually do not see the dividend discussion surface until around three years after the captive year ended. The captive board will review the captive's financial situation when it comes to equity versus liabilities (loss reserves) and may or may not declare a dividend at that point. Just so you are aware, even if all claims happen to be closed, there is still IBNR to deal with as well as the potential for a claim to reopen, particularly in the world of workers' compensation. Because of this, it is more customary for the captive board to declare a partial dividend after three years, then possibly additional dividends in later years until such time that the future obligations are taken care of.

However, remember, if a claim continues to grow, or reopens and settles for $1,000,000, the captive still has reinsurance will step in and assume any payments on that claim. Therefore, once a claim exceeds the captive's reinsurance threshold, it no longer has to worry about future liabilities surrounding that claim. The delay is mainly due to IBNR and possibility of smaller claims becoming larger.

After five, six or seven years we typically see that somewhere between 90% or 95% of potential dividends have been paid out. Obviously, business owners do not want to wait forever for their equity. Typically, there are three ways to deal with future liability: Internal Loss Tail Fund, Commutation, and Novation.

Internal Loss Tail Fund

Captive have been using this process for decades. The captive manager and actuary will, together, calculate and create an internal tail fund. Basically, at some point in the future, typically five, six, or seven years after the end of a captive year, they roll the liability of that captive program year to a current program year.

The premium for that tail fund, as well as the liabilities for future claims payment, is rolled forward to the current year. Once completed, this enables the captive to close that program year and declare a final dividend.

Rolling the tail fund forward is like selling it to the future year. That future year receives the actuarial calculated reserves and funds for IBNR reserves. After seven years, the possibility of having a claim pop up that was not known previously is rather remote, but still statistically possible. If the claims settle out for less than actuarially calculated, that future year makes additional profit. If it does not settle for less, the difference would be shared by the members of the captive in that future year based on a percentage of their premium paid in. Also, keep in mind, that there is still reinsurance for any large claim that does actually pop up. Therefore, the group should be able to absorb any amount with minimal impact to each member.

Commutation

A commutation is similar to that of an Internal Loss Tail Fund but instead of the captive actuary doing the calculation, the Fronting Insurance Company's actuaries calculate the reserves and funds for IBNR reserves, plus add in a margin for potential error as well as return on investment. The Fronting Insurance Company would then assume all the future liabilities for that year. The captive sells their liabilities to the Fronting Insurance Company. The Fronting Insurance Company is viewing it as an investment, and since the Fronting Insurance Company is legally obligated for all claims that the captive does not pay, they can easily assume the future claims.

Novation

A Novation is identical to that of a Commutation in that the captive is selling its future liabilities, but in this case, instead of the claims being sold to the related Fronting Insurance Company, they are sold to a third party. The complexity with that is that the Fronting Insurance Company is still legally obligated for all claims that the captive does not pay. Therefore, the Fronting Insurance Company must accept the third party that is assuming the captive's liabilities.

Once the future liabilities of the captive are finalized, the captive board is free to declare a final dividend of the rest of the proceeds to the members: underwriting profit and investment income.

Captive Ownership

Even though a business is insured by a captive, it does not mean that the business needs to be the owner of the captive. In fact, in middle market businesses, it is more likely that the ownership of the captive is held by the owners of the business. In some cases, when a business owner wants to deal with Estate issues, they may have the captive owned by their trust or by their heirs. We have also seen where a business owner may reward a key individual with partial ownership in the captive; therefore, the key person would receive a potential bonus without the employer having to pay for it separately.

Why not the business own the captive? The owner of the captive is the one that receives any dividend proceeds from a captive. Therefore, it is a way to transfer monies from a business to the individual owner(s) of the captive without passing through the business. In the case of a group captive, the dividend would most likely be viewed as ordinary income, but in the case of an 831(b) captive, it would most likely be viewed as a capital gains. You have to remember that different captive structures and methods of ownership have different tax ramifications.

Exiting a Captive

Discussing only all the benefits of a captive and how to join it without also discussing exiting would be unfair and unwise.

Even though business owners look at going into a captive as a long-term investment, exiting a captive can occur at the end of any captive program year. You can make a decision to leave for business purposes at each anniversary, however, your obligations to the captive do not end until the last year you participated in a captive year closes out. At the program year closure, your capitalization costs and collateral would be returned to you, and your obligation ends. As we already went through how dividends are declared, and programs years close out, it will typically be five, six or seven years before your last potential dividend, collateral and capitalization are returned to you.

Typically, three or four years after the program year ends, you will pretty much know what will be your situation moving forward. After three of four years, that program year's fluctuations in reserves and results usually do not change much.

———

Employee Health Insurance Captives

A practice that has existed for decades, the use of a captive for employee health insurance coverages, has exploded in recent years as employers seek to overcome the affects that rising health insurance premiums have had on their bottom lines. Employers have been moving to captives, particularly group captives, for a multitude of reasons, think of the **Five C's**: Control, Claims, Coverage, Compliance, and Cost.

Control

Employers have the feeling that they have no control over their health insurance program, how their employees use the health insurance, and how claim costs are contained. The use of a captive for employee health insurance gives an employer the ability to take back control as you will discover as we explore the rest of the C's.

Claims

Unlike when you are fully insured, you will have easy access to your claims data. You may be able to receive some data from your traditional insurance company if you are large enough of a client that they are willing to provided it, however they usually do so reluctantly and with delays. In a captive, you will readily receive your claim information. It will not be employee specific, but you will be able to see what employees are being treated for, or diagnosed with, in general. That way, you can establish wellness programs to try and combat areas that may raise your healthcare utilization and therefore your premiums. It is simple risk management; if you see issues that are causing claims, you put programs in place to mitigate the impact of those issues, or better yet, put programs in place to prevent things from occurring, or at least occur less frequently and with less severity. This is where Employee Wellness programs can have an impact.

Coverage

Being part of a captive, you are able to customize your insurance coverage program. You will not be restricted to one specific insurance company's network, you will able to choose a network, or networks, you want from a multitude of options. This will allow you to choose based on locations, medical providers, or discounts available within a network.

You can also customize the coverage to control costs. If you see too many people using emergency room services, which are far more expensive, you can change your employee co-pay in the middle of the program year to a higher co-pay to dissuade them from doing so. If you see too many chiropractic visits, you can set limitations. The ability to restrict coverage to control costs, so long as you are still compliant with regulations, you will be able to do so. You can make these mid-program year changes by simply giving your employees written notice of the change.

Compliance

Your captive manager, or broker, will make sure you are compliant with current regulations so you do not need worry about this. If you are self-insured, you must undergo Department of Labor exemptions for the ERISA benefits, the same would apply to the use of a single-parent captive. The Department of Labor still views a single-parent captive as being self-insured with regards to ERISA compliance. In both cases, your captive manager or broker, will assist you with compliance. On the other hand, if you are participating with a group health insurance captive, you do not need to file for exemption to meet that ERISA requirements.

Cost

As you can see, a captive has all the advantages of self-insurance when it comes to cost control, and if you are in a group captive, you have less regulatory compliance to worry about. However, there are additional benefits with a captive.

Right out of the gate, a health insurance captive has the benefit of being viewed as a self-insurance program, and therefore exempt from the Affordable Care Act (ACA) Insurer Premium Fee (Tax) assessed to all health insurance companies does not apply. What started out in 2014 as an $8,000,000,000 (yes, that is $8 Billion) ACA assessment fee to all health insurance companies, increases to $13.9 Billion in 2017, and will be indexed upwards from there. This ACA fee is applied to all health insurance companies based on a percentage of their premium written in the entire USA marketplace for traditional health insurance (not self-insured). As everyone knows, this fee is clearly being passed on to employers using their traditional insurance company programs.

Second, cash flow is more predictable. In the self-insured world, you must pay your claims as incurred, so if a number of employees seek service in one month, or an employee has a significant healthcare event, you would have to pay for those service costs, up to your stop-loss points, at one time. Therefore, one month may be a small payment and another large. With a group captive, can pay in monthly as the group would most likely be able to spread the claims payments over more employers so all you may have is your normal monthly premium payments.

Third, just as we discussed before, insurance companies make more profit from insuring the smaller, predictable and controllable claims than they do from covering the unexpected, catastrophic claims. Using captives, a single employer, or group of employers, can self-insure their smaller, more predictable claims and then utilize reinsurance, also known as Stop Loss Coverage in the health insurance world, to cover the unexpected, catastrophic claims. This allows the employer(s) to receive the potential underwriting and investment income back in the form of a dividend.

There two significant differences between health insurance captives and captives that provide general liability and workers' compensation coverages: the claim runoff period and the funding for losses.

Claim Runoff Period

The claim runoff period used in healthcare captives is significantly different than those insuring liabilities. We discussed that in when you insure liability claims, that it may take years for them to be reported (remember IBNR) or settled. In the health insurance captive world, the captive is paying the claims as services are incurred, therefore there is no long period needed for claim reporting, development, settlement, or even IBNR.

For example, if you see your doctor on December 28th of 2016, and the bill arrives on February 1st of 2017, the 2016 program year of the captive takes care of the bill. Your follow-up visit on January 2nd that you also received the bill for on February 1st would be paid in the 2017 program year. All treatments, physician visits, prescriptions filled that occurred during a captive program year are paid by that captive year.

As you can quickly see, in health insurance, there is no long timeframe that you have to wait to see if or when a "claim" is made, or how long it will take to settle an issue in court. Therefore, there is no need for a five to seven-year captive program year closure timeframe. Healthcare captive programs typically have a three to six month claim run-off period where they do wait for the bill for services rendered during that program year. After that very short claim run-off period, a dividend will be declared.

Health Insurance Loss Fund

In a captive that insured things such as workers' compensation and liability, it is common for the loss fund for a business be set at the predicted loss amount, as we discussed, the Initial Loss Fund. In those captive, it is also common to have a stipulation that there be an amount that the business may also have to pay should the claims of the individual company exceed a certain amount, the Potential Loss Fund. These two combine to be the total maximum loss funding before the maximum aggregate retention point is reached and the excess reinsurance starts to pay for the claims. The funding for such a captive was outlined in Chapter 2-What is a Captive.

In a Health Insurance Captive, it is possible to fund to the maximum aggregate retention. Funding your loss fund in this matter provides two benefits: first, collateral requirements will be reduced as the captive should have enough funds to pay for a worst-case scenario; and second, since the likelihood of the aggregate payments that the captive has to pay for its retained claims is very unlikely, this makes it common to have underwriting profit and therefore dividends are frequently paid.

Based on everything outlined here, you can see why health insurance captives have become so popular. They typically are very competitive in terms of the premiums being paid upfront as compared to traditional health insurance, they can return underwriting profit dividends, and can provide the ability to control your plan more to your needs.

An additional note: There is a perception that your HR department will have an increased burden of work (and anxiety) when it comes to administering a self-insured or captive program. In reality, with today's technology, the integration between your network(s) and your third-party claims administrator will feel more like a traditional health insurance company than you realize. Plus, your captive manager or broker should be able to assist in the administration and changeover. However, just as with changing any healthcare insurance company, you will still need to go through the process initially of changing "insurance providers".

831(b) Enterprise Risk Captives

Over 90 percent of Fortune 1000 companies and many successful middle market businesses have 831(b) Enterprise Risk Captives. The name 831(b) Captive comes from the actual US tax code provision that was enacted as part of the 1986 Tax Reform Act enacted by Congress and signed by President Ronald Reagan into law during his 2nd term – *U.S. Code, Title 26, Subtitle A, Chapter 1, Subchapter L, Part II, section 831, subsection (b), of the United States Internal Revenue Code, titled "Alternative tax for certain small companies."*

Theses 831(b) Captives, are also referred to as "Micro-Captives", "Mini-Captives" or "Enterprise Risk Captives", and are used by profitable, cash flow positive mid-size companies looking for cost-effective ways to finance and transfer risk that the traditional insurance marketplace cannot "insure". When properly structured, there are numerous benefits of owning an 831(b) Captive including possible financial, estate and tax advantages, such as:

- it provides a business the means to accumulate a loss fund, in a tax favorable way, to provide the liquidity to pay for a loss that may not normally be insurable in the traditional insurance marketplace,

- premiums paid by the business to the captive would be a legitimate, tax deductible expense,

- the 831(b) Captive pays no Federal income tax on the premium collected but the captive company makes an election at its inception to pay tax *only* on its investment income,

- the underwriting profits of the captive may be returned to the captive owner(s) as a capital gain instead of ordinary income, and

- the captive may be owned by the individual owner(s) of a business, or by others not related to the business including family members.

From the benefits above, you can see why the use of an 831(b) Captive is one of the most popular choices for middle market companies to help manage their risks. However, there are limitations to the captive: the captive will have maximum annual premium limitation of $2,200,000; and the captive cannot directly pay a third party, it can only reimburse the insured business for covered losses that occur. Because of these limitations, it is predominantly used to insure risks that no traditional insurance company will cover, or to fill holes in an existing traditional insurance program.

Let us step aside for a moment to understand "Traditional Insurance", which is simply the transfer of risk from the insured business to the insurance company. It takes many forms including: auto, general liability, property, workers' compensation, professional liability and many more. What makes the transaction "traditional"? An insurance agent submits their client's underwriting applications and financial information, the insurance company evaluates the risk to be insured (for example in Property insurance the underwriter considers COPE-- Construction-Occupancy or use—Protection available—Exposures). When that information is understood, the underwriter uses their available filed rates determine the appropriate pricing for the policy. When the policy is issued, and delivered to the business, the business has shifted their risk of loss from themselves to the insurance company via the payment of the premium. If the loss that occurs is described in the insuring conditions of the insurance policy purchased, the insurance company is now fully responsible for paying that loss.

The types of risk listed above are rather typical, and depending upon the business, they face at least some of these risks as a statutory requirement. (example: workers' compensation, auto liability, general liability, professional liability, etc.).

However, there are innumerable other kinds of exposure and risks that your business faces in your daily work activity that you may, or may not, recognize as being a threat to your success and perhaps your future existence. Various other types of risks include, but are certainly not limited to the following:

- **Political risks** — civil unrest, terrorism, war or intentional violent acts
- **Regulatory** — unintentional loss of personal or business licenses, statute changes
- **Contingent Liabilities** — weather, lack of materials or manpower
- **Trade Credit** — diminution of values, accounts receivable
- **Business** — loss of a key client, franchise or supplier relationship; loss of Bonding Capacity; material price fluctuations
- **Financial Risk** — interest rate fluctuations, foreign exchange rate fluctuations
- **Reputation** — brand value, key person and/or corporate image
- **Competition** — price wars
- **Service Contracts** — furniture, appliances, autos, equipment, homes
- **Non-ERISA Medical Plan losses** — HRA's
- **Large Deductible Losses** — workers comp, medical plan, liability

The types of exposure noted above truly only "scratch the surface" of what a business may protect from loss through the use of an 831(b) Captive. You may also think of numerous other risks that are not typically insurable, or perhaps not affordable, through the commercial markets. One way to identify risks that are not being traditionally insured by you is to open your liability and property insurance policies and read what is describe as not being covered (such as paved surfaces, bridges, or underground property) or specifically excluded (such as your product, your work, or intentional acts of an employee).

Most of those exposures may be insured non-traditionally with an alternative market approach such as an 831(b) captive.

When you consider a new way of thinking about risk, the two critical issues that must be accomplished are the identification of the risk, then the quantification and rating of the risk by the underwriter and actuary. If a premium can be actuarially developed and defended, the risk can then be insured, whether commercially or non-traditionally.

Important Note

831(b) Captives must be properly managed and structured or they will get themselves in trouble. This is important as there are 831(b) Captive Promoters that have not structured the 931(b) Captives properly, and therefore those captives were viewed by the IRS as being a self-insurance program. As we reviewed before, with self-insurance programs, only claim expenses are viewed as a legitimate, tax deductible expense and not the reserves and premiums paid.

Because of these promoters, there have been IRS and court challenges to some 831(b) Captive programs. However, if you follow the rules and regulations properly, the captives that have done so have typically prevailed. Each case must be carefully evaluated, for the lack of proper management and structuring will disqualify the 831(b) Captive from the correct tax treatment afforded by the IRS code.

The critical issues that an 831(b) Captive insurance programs will face scrutiny of are **Capitalization, Risk Transfer, Risk Distribution, Actuarial Soundness,** and **Use of Life Insurance**.

Capitalization

Like any other insurance company or captive, an 831(b) Captive must be appropriately capitalized at its inception, and must be professionally operated and managed. These requirements will be established by the regulations of the state or country in which the captive is domiciled.

The biggest issue is that the captive must be able to pay the claims that may and do occur, therefore it must collect and hold premiums to pay those claims, it must have reserves and surplus. This might sound strange, but there have been "paper" 831(b) Captives that were created, businesses wrote off the premiums, but never actually paid the premiums. Or, they paid the premiums the last day of the calendar year, and declared a dividend the first of the following year, so the captive never really collected and held any premiums.

An 831(b) Captive will also carry an election to be a U.S. Taxpayer. Even though the captive may be domiciled in a foreign country, the funds can and will be held inside the U.S. but will be owned by the captive. Not doing so will subject yourself to Federal Excise Tax (a tax imposed on premium payments to offshore insurers: 4 percent on direct premiums and 1 percent on reinsurance premiums) and most likely additional IRS scrutiny.

Risk Transfer

There must be clear, documented transfer of the risk from the operating company to the insurance company. The risk transfer is accomplished via the issuance of an insurance policy, with actuarially determined premiums and a clear set of insuring conditions and policy terms. If you do not have sound insurance policies provided by the captive, it will not be viewed as a legitimate purchase of insurance.

Risk Distribution

The insurance company needs to have third party business (unaffiliated to the single operating company) within the insurance company's written premium. In other words, if you have no risk of losing some of your captive funds to an unrelated business' claim, your captive will not be viewed as an insurance company, it will be viewed as self-insurance. At the time of the writing of this book, there was no specific regulation that determines the required level of third party business, though most insurance professionals focus on levels ranging between 30% to 50% of the total written premium of the company.

Third party business may be acquired in a number of ways, including the pooling of various exposures with other captives, simply purchasing unrelated insurance business from other carriers and even some insurance policies that the captive may issue might qualify as unrelated business.

For example, there are many retailers that sell Extended Warranties on their products and utilize an 831(b) Captive to finance those risks. Keep in mind, that although warranties are third party risks, warranties are not "insurance" in many U.S. jurisdictions and therefore will most likely require you to use a foreign domicile for such risks.

Actuarial Soundness

We touched on previously that if a premium can be actuarially developed and defended, the risk can then be insured by an 831(b) Captive. However, if your maximum probable exposure to a loss is $100,000, you cannot actuarily justify a $500,000 premium. Like other insurance policies you purchase, the maximum loss that you may face should be greater than the premium you pay.

Also, yes, you can insure exposures in your 831(b) Captive that may be able to be traditionally insured as you view the risk small enough that you want to self-insure it. A good rule of thumb in those cases, the premium you pay should me comparable what you can purchase it for in the traditional marketplace. For example, purchasing Cyber Insurance in your captive may make sense, but if the actuary determines the premium to be $20,000 for $1,000,000 of coverage, and you can purchase the same coverage for $10,000, that may be okay as it is similar, however, I have seen some provide that coverage in their captive at a premium of $100,000 or more.

Use of Life Insurance

As 831(b) captives pay taxes on investment income, the IRS will frown on the use of cash value life insurance as an investment by a captive as life insurance investments grow tax free.

Some 831(b) Captive promoters use this tactic as they can make it sound very attractive to someone. Face it, some promoters (that is not looking out for your best interest) will state that you can pay for the life insurance on a pre-tax basis, that it will be a way to accumulate funds from being taxed, and possibly even that you can take a loan from the cash value to avoid paying income tax. All of this sounds attractive, however, it will cause your 831(b) to be viewed by the IRS as nothing but a tax shelter. Remember, if it sounds too good to be true, it probably is. These promoters are selling this concept to you as they will receive a big commission when placing the life insurance policy.

Now, after reading all of this, you might be thinking that the federal government does not like 831(b) captives, that is not the case. In fact, congress passed the 2015 Appropriations Bill under the Obama Administration that actually increase the maximum allowable premium for an 831(b) Captive from $1,200,000 to $2,200,000. The Federal Government clearly understands the need for and benefits of a properly structure 831(b) Captive, they are simply trying to keep the use of these from being abused.

———

Benchmarking Performance

As you now understand, the more risk you take on yourself, the lower your cost of risk, i.e. your insurance cost. However, never take that huge step into the alternative risk financing world, or any change beyond guaranteed cost, unless you conduct an analysis and *fully* understand your risk-reward. You also need to understand the cash flow implications and collateral requirements of each model, so that ultimately you achieve your goal of dramatically reducing your costs.

One of the things I have seen in alternative risk financing programs, such as high deductible, captives, and self-insured, is many employers go into them assuming they are going to reduce their overall cost of insurance. But their downfall may be that their house is not order. When you actually calculate, and analyze their costs, they may still be paying too much. The cause of higher costs could be the frequency and/or severity of claims caused by a lack of attention to the entire risk management cycle as they are focused on other things going on in their organization.

Case in point: I met the CFO of a multi-state retail store chain at a conference in which I was a speaker. He came up to me after my session and asked why I believed that the experience modifier could also be used as a benchmark in determining how well one is managing their risks. He stated that experience modifiers do not really apply to his company, since his company was in a captive, and modifiers really do not have an impact on his premium. It turned out that in each state of operation, his company suffered with surcharged experience modifiers.

I agreed with him that insurance costs will normally be lower in a captive than guaranteed cost coverage. However, I then questioned why his company, in comparison to their peers, was still having a higher frequency or severity of claims, and therefore still paying too much out in terms of "insurance costs." He responded that he had not considered it in this light. He believed his company was getting the lowest premium using a captive versus a guaranteed-cost program. However, he did not fully realize his company was still paying too much because of the claims they were still having. The company was not where it could be if its house had been in order and their claims under control. In other words, his false sense of lower costs in a captive was keeping him from seeing that he was still dipping into his checkbook far more than he should have.

As I previously mentioned about retrospectively-rated programs, an alternative financing program can be used to mask a problem. Even though you may be in alternative financing, you need to continually analyze and benchmark your results. You must compare yourself with your peers and with other organizations, plus determine what your experience modifier would be if you were not self-insured.

It is this continual process of benchmarking and monitoring your performance that determines whether you achieve your ultimate goal of paying the lowest possible insurance costs. Make certain problems are not being masked by your program design, thus causing you to waste significant dollars that could be better used elsewhere within your organization.

It is important to determine whether you are doing a good, fair or bad job. Are you improving or trending in the wrong direction? There are certain data points we suggest every executive analyze every year, so you can benchmark your progress. These can be complied into what we refer to as *Your Annual Executive Briefing*.

Your Annual Executive Briefing includes:

- *Your Work Comp Experience Modifier Analysis* – Even though your premium is based on your five years of claims, and not your modifier directly, your modifier is also a snapshot of three of those same years.
  - *Minimum Modifier* – This is your modifier if you had *zero* claims. If you do not know this, how can you

benchmark how much extra money your claims are costing you?

- o *Controllable Experience Modifier* – The gap between your current experience modifier and your desired, minimum experience modifier. It gives you a ballpark as to how much your claims are costing you.

- o *Actual Losses versus Expected Losses* – Are you doing better or worse than average? This report shows you a year by year comparison of how much your claim dollars are in comparison to what the rating bureau expected based on your reported payrolls.

- *Net Rates versus Exposures* – If you take your premium by type of policy and compare that to the rating basis you can determine your net rate. For example, your workers' compensation premium divided by your total payroll, your general liability premium divided by total revenue (or payroll), and auto premium divided by the number of power units. When you compare this year by year, you can see if you are trending up, down or flat.

- *Injury Statistics* – The use of OSHA statistics is very good as OSHA has statistics for every type of business. Therefore, you can compare yourself to your peers, as well as to yourself over time. Items you may want to record and benchmark might include OSHA Recordable and DART rates (Days Away, Restricted Duty, or Transitional Duty). You should also include items such as near misses and observed unsafe actions that did not result in an injury or property damage, but were "near misses." Keep in mind that OSHA recordable, DART and near misses should all have specific numeric goals established that reduce over time. This way you can determine the success of your program.

- *Observation Statistics* – These can be established based upon your business and items you determine are best measured. It could be reporting by peers or supervisors of observed improper actions, defective parts counts, product or work that does not meet quality standards, consumer complaints, or cost of reworked jobs.

Observed statistics should not have specific numeric goals of being reduced over time. This may sound contradictory, but we have seen supervisors not record such incidents as they were afraid that they may be reprimanded, lose their job or a bonus, because they are not observing fewer unsafe actions. Remember, the goal is to prevent the injury or poor-quality work, not just to make the paperwork look good. Therefore, any and all improper actions need reporting, even if no injuries or close calls occur, so that potential problem areas or employees can be addressed before something serious occurs.

- *Automotive & Safer Reports* – The Federal Motor Carrier Safety Administration keeps statistics on its website of any DOT operation. They track inspections that lead to Vehicle, Driver or Hazmat Out of Service percentages, as well as unsafe driving, crashes, maintenance and other statistics that you can compare yourself to your peers as well as to yourself.

    You can also invest in a Telematics system for your fleet. Telematics can help track and minimize risk with real-time insights that improve driving, reduce claims and maximize productivity. Using secure website and smart phone app so fleet managers can get real-time insights on fuel consumption, vehicle health, location, driver safety and more. Knowing drivers' habits and whereabouts throughout the day can help managers to optimize routes, maximize productivity, save money and increase safety measures. You can use reports to measure your fleet in both real-time as well as over a period of time.

Benchmark your results. If you do not measure it, you cannot determine if you are doing a good job or not. You must focus long term to earn an "A" on your modifier report card.

Senior management must track and measure various components to hold the supervisors accountable. Yes, even the executives of the organization must monitor those below them to establish the supervisor is doing his or her job. Nothing undoes a safety or quality control program quicker than a supervisor who is only focused on productivity with no regard for safety or quality.

Establish a line of communication for feedback from bottom to top. In other words, if an employee feels their supervisor is ignoring a situation that has been brought to their attention, they must feel safe that they can go above their supervisor without fear of repercussions and know who they can go to in such a circumstance.

———————

Leveraging Risk Management

In the captive world, the actuary will determine your loss fund and your premium based on the risk of your operations and the losses or claims that you have incurred. They will review the data provided to them to perform the actuarial analysis.

However, they will also want the data regarding any changes you have implemented within your operations that have led to improvement in your data. For example, if you have had some bad injuries several years ago, and three years ago you hired a safety manager and implemented changes that are evident in the most recent years, the actuary can adjust their formulas or thinking accordingly.

As you can see, your premium is derived by what the actuary and underwriter perceive to be the risk of your organization, namely your *Risk Profile*. To help you visualize how an underwriter looks at your business in order to calculate your Risk Profile and to determine the premium they will charge to insure you as a risk, I created the following conceptual premium formula:

| Your claim costs over 5 years | + | Perception of additional potential risks and claims | − | Perception of how much you improved your risk and addressed claims over the past year(s) | = | **Your Risk Profile and Premium** |

So, what is your Risk Profile?

When you take time to improve your Risk Profile and reduce your risks, you will ultimately drive down your insurance costs. When you reduce your risks, you improve your safety and quality of your operations, which will reduce the frequency and severity of injuries and accidents. When you reduce your risks, you improve quality control and your policies and procedures, which will reduce the number of incidents and lawsuits. Everything we are discussing revolves around what the perception of your Risk Profile is.

The effect of Risk Profile on premiums is not only evident in captives, it is very evident in traditional insurance as well. You may be thinking of the insurance agents that come in and focus on the financing of your risk or insurance by asking "Can we quote you?", when what they really mean is "Can we find holes and gaps to cover your risk and basically up sell you?". I believe you are beginning to see more clearly why I believe the traditional insurance shopping, or quoting process, is not truly beneficial to you as an employer.

Captives and your focus on Risk Management will help you get out of the quote and hope trap, and the poor results that come from that trap. It takes years for claims that have already occurred to appear on your loss runs, falling outside the *"Your claim costs over five years"* window most underwriters look at. Therefore, the quickest and best way to reduce your rates in both the short and long term is to focus on impacting the underwriter's *"Perception of how much you improved your risk and addressed claims over the past year(s),"* and you can only do so by focusing on the entire Risk Management Process.

The Risk Management Process is a five-step ongoing process that involves:

- Risk Identification
- Risk Analysis
- Risk Control
- Risk Transfer and Implementation
- Risk Review and Refinement

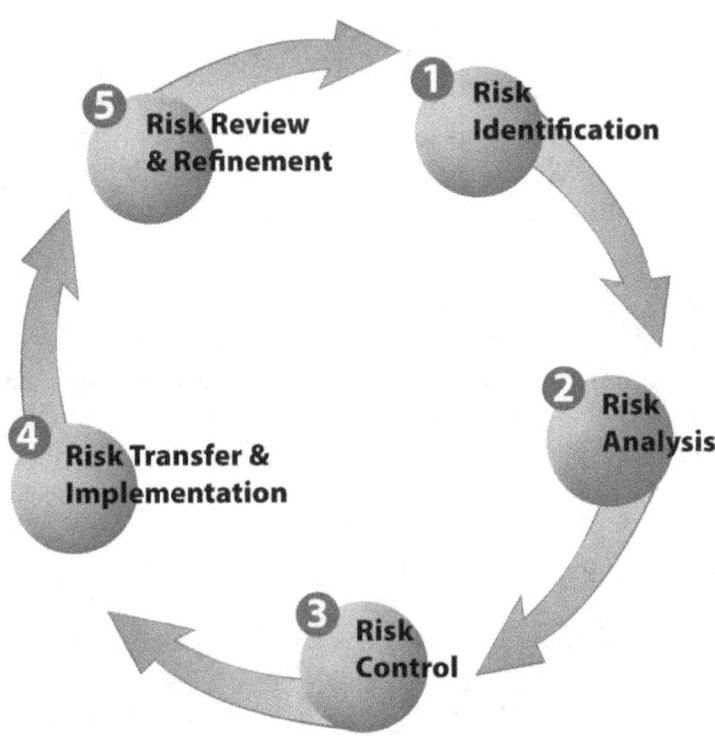

As you now realize, many insurance agents jump directly into step four, risk transfer and implementation, by quoting your insurance and transferring that risk to an insurance company. Sadly, they do not spend the time in the risk identification phase. (We will discuss more on what the agent's role should be in Chapter 14.)

Yes, agents may identify some exposures or things that could be potential claims, but their focus is to try to sell you coverage. If, ultimately, you are going to buy coverage, whether it is for primary coverage or to cover excess losses if you are self-insured or in a captive, you are going to pay a premium based on your risk. If you are bidding out your insurance and have not addressed your risks, you may have purchased coverage at the "best" quote that year, but you are actually going to pay a higher premium based on the perception of a higher risk, and pay a higher premium than if things were put in place to control that risk. The question really is: if you control risk well enough, does it make financial sense to even purchase insurance coverage for that risk? Or as you can now see, is it better to insure that in a captive?

As we go through the steps of the Risk Management Process, it may be easiest to understand the complete process by providing you with a general overview of how my team goes through this entire process when working with our clients. There is no right or wrong way to go through the process, but do not skimp on the process. Make sure you go through each and every step thoroughly.

Step One: Risk Identification

During this step, you really need to dig in and identify all the risks inside your organization. Our initial Risk Management and HR Assessment is a lengthy process, but not overwhelming to our clients as we probably spend eight or nine times the number of hours that our clients spend in the process. It is a critical initial step because if we do not identify the risks and gather good data, we cannot analyze it and figure out how to best control it. Also, we cannot determine how to best deal with this information through either better controls, making a transfer, buying insurance, etc. Let us jump ahead a little. If we decide we are going to buy insurance for this risk, we cannot clearly explain to an underwriter how we improved this risk if we have not first identified it and understood it.

When we work with our clients, we invest hours gathering and analyzing data. Steps include a thorough loss analysis, looking at OSHA logs, and interviewing key employees to better understand exactly what the risks are that they see in the organization. We then go through their current safety programs, their compliance, their claims reporting and management process, their quality control procedures, and their HR including hiring and orientation process. We also tour and analyze the facility or job sites. We do all of this so we can fully understand a particular business thoroughly, and to be able to identify the risks associated with it.

In this stage, it is important to be open and honest with yourself or with an outsourced risk manager about your entire organization and its inner workings. If you do not identify the risks, you cannot address the risks. Ignoring or trying to hide a risk is equivalent to sticking your head in the sand and hoping something bad does not happen.

I became friends with a business owner, who loves to tell me sayings and stories he learned from his dad and granddad. One of the first sayings he conveyed to me when I met him was that his dad always told him, *"Keep his insurance agents like mushrooms – in the dark and feed them sh##!."* When we first met, his premiums were exploding. What he came to realize at that time was that hiding things caught up to him as eventually insurance companies did see what he was not openly sharing about his company. Ultimately, insurance companies and actuaries will see your risks through your loss runs, or they will see the risks during a loss control inspection of your business. Either way, you will pay premiums according to those risks.

When we dig into your operation, we are going to be conducting a five-year or more *Loss Analysis* of your incidents. This applies to your entire organization, including workers' compensation, general and auto liability, property, etc. We are looking for the totality of the risks that impact your business. For example, a poor fleet safety program or experiencing frequent fleet losses is important because vehicular accidents can injure your employees and damage products being delivered.

We are going to look at five years of OSHA logs (OSHA 300's and 300A's), as well as your accident/incident and near miss investigation reports. We are going to look through your employee handbook, go through and review your safety manuals, fleet safety program, safety committee and training schedule notes, as well as your policies and procedures. We will understand how you hire new employees and review your employment application, employment packet, how you orient your employees, and how you conduct your safety programs and how often.

Conducting a *Loss Analysis* will enable us to determine the origin of claims and injuries, what are the causes and types of claims, and eventually this will allow us to know where to begin our focus on prevention. By understanding what changes or processes you implement following those claims, we can see the holes or problems in your policies, procedures and programs. We will determine if you have problems with individual employees who are frequent claim repeaters or causes of claims, or a possible problem area of your operations. We may have them go through a program specifically directed at reducing the potential of a repeater becoming injured again.

We conduct an *Experience Modifier Analysis*, where we look at your experience modifier worksheets to understand how your experience modifier was calculated and to verify if it is even correct. We can then determine what is needed to improve your injury management and return-to-work processes so we can improve your future modifier calculations. What I find interesting is that occasionally we even find claims reported on a company's modifier that were from another company. If so, then you are being overcharged in this case.

Even a thorough *Coverage Analysis*, a review of your insurance policies, is important. Believe it or not, your insurance policies are a good place to understand some of your risks. The insurance company has identified certain risks they are listing, scheduling, or covering on your policy. For example, we understand how many, what type and size (weight) of vehicles you have, and even their use through their classification codes. These are all on your policy. Based on the size and nature of your fleet, how you control the selection of drivers and conduct fleet safety will be critical to your overall Risk Profile.

It is interesting that in addition to identifying risks and adding endorsements to your policy to add specific coverage for those risks, the insurance company may have also identified specific risks and added an exclusion to the policy because it is a risk they do not want to cover. I cannot even count how many times we have conducted a *Coverage Analysis* and seen policy exclusion endorsements relating to something material in a business' operation. In these situations, the insurance company identified a risk, determined they were uncomfortable with how the risk was being addressed, and decided to exclude coverage.

A *Contract Analysis* of your contracts and leases is also necessary. It is important to understand what risks you have contractually taken on as well as those you are attempting to transfer to others. This is especially true of those that you have signed that may not actually be "insurable".

In addition, an analysis of your past insurance company's surveys and recommendations, and your responses can shed some light on what risks you are facing.

Even a *Fleet Safety Analysis* of your DOT and audits, or safety reports, driver screening and eligibility criteria, and employee training and monitoring records are items that should be reviewed if you have employees driving on the roads.

With every business, we will also conduct a *Facility and/or Job Site Analysis*. When touring a facility or a job site, we can see everything you do in action. We can see your housekeeping, your safety, your maintenance, your quality controls, how you produce your revenue, and how well your employees perform.

The entire goal is to eventually help better identify your risk and minimize or eliminate the issues to ultimately drive down your costs and increase your profitability over expenses. After all this information is gathered through employee interviews, through data and coverage loss assessment and analysis, we dig in and conduct a risk analysis.

In Appendix B, you will find a list of the items that typically would be looked at as part of a Risk Identification process. There are also checklists available online that you can use to help in the Risk Identification process.

Step Two: Risk Analysis

After developing a thorough understanding of your business, your industry, your corporate culture, your operating procedures, and the risks your operation faces, you are starting to move beyond insurance and towards Risk Profile improvement. In the Risk Analysis stage, we determine the potential impact of those identified risks by measuring and prioritizing them so you can determine if it makes sense to address a certain risk now or later, and eventually how much time, money and effort should be spent on dealing with a certain risk.

Risk Analysis & Prioritization Scale

Severity	High	III	IV
	Low	I	II
		Low	High
		Frequency	

You should place each risk in one of the above four category grids. The vertical is the severity of the impact of the risk; the horizontal is the likely frequency the risk may occur.

Risks in Box IV are going to have the biggest potential impact on the operation and deserve first priority. Focus on risks in Box III and II next. Those risks in Box I are a low priority.

Step Three: Risk Control

During the risk control phase, we determine which programs and processes are most effective to reduce the frequency and/or severity of that risk, and ultimately reduce the total cost of risk on the organization.

You need to take the time to understand and analyze each risk you identified. When it comes to determining how best to control the risk, it is cost versus benefit for an organization. The goal is to have controls in place for a risk, which then enables you to move that risk from Box IV to a lower risk category of either Box III or II. Eventually, you want to have programs and processes in place to move as many risks down in category from III to II, or II to I, and eventually as many of those risks to that of Box I as you can.

In a bit more detail, you would likely retain a small infrequent risk that rarely occurs and has very little consequence to it. Why pay insurance premiums to cover this small probable risk? You would not need to spend much time addressing or controlling this risk. Whereas, if that small risk occurs frequently and consistently, you would focus on determining the best way to control the risk by preventing it from occurring or reducing the frequency of the occurrence. Eventually you may want to retain that risk versus paying an insurance company to insure it.

On the other hand, if you have a risk of great significance it is obviously something you would not retain. You must purchase insurance or reinsurance for this risk. Remember, the insurance company is charging you a premium based on their perception of this risk. Therefore, dig into the risk and figure out how best to control it by reducing the potential severity and its likelihood of occurring.

Explore a spectrum of proven alternative strategies to minimize a risk. Whether it is behavior-based safety, training education, physically changing a job, transferring (subcontracting) the risk contractually to another party or even avoiding the risk all together, the goal is to improve your Risk Profile and perception of risk, and dramatically reduce your insurance costs.

Step Four: Risk Transfer and Implementation

Once you complete these steps, then it is time to implement the risk control programs and processes geared at reducing the frequency and/or severity of losses, and then conduct your risk transfer. The implementation process consists of specifically tailored programs and strategies designed to reduce those risks, which ultimately will lead to reduced insurance costs. In fact, if you reduce a particular risk enough, you may be in a position where buying insurance for that risk no longer makes financial sense. Retaining a particular risk via self-insurance or a captive may enable you to save money you would have paid to insure that risk.

Once you implement these programs and processes, it is time to implement your negotiating advantage in the insurance marketplace. You will now be able to better leverage how you have improved your Risk Profile. It is the minus in the equation, the perception of how much you have improved your risk over the past year or years. You need to clearly and precisely convey to the insurance companies the improvements you have undertaken that will ultimately drive down the rates that they are charging.

This is also the time to look at insurance programs. You would also want to look at alternative financing arrangements which we reviewed in the first two chapters, such as the use of captives.

You may not realize it but this is the point where most insurance agents start the process and focus on trying to sell you coverage to make a commission. However, in comparison, we are in the fourth step of a process to improve your Risk Profile, which will ultimately yield better results.

Step Five: Risk Review and Refinement

At step five, we evaluate the effectiveness of your risk management programs, practices and resources under real-world conditions to make certain the programs and processes work correctly. Remember, risk management is an *ongoing* process. You must continue to determine if your programs are working. If not, then adjust them. You also want to identify new risks, analyze and control them by implementing new programs. If you do not control your risks, you are susceptible to the risks controlling you.

The whole idea behind Risk Profile Improvement is to go through the entire Risk Management process cycle and continue to do so. How do you know if your insurance program is adequate and meets your needs if you do not go through the entire Risk Profile Improvement Process and the Risk Management Cycle?

We will talk about agent selection in Chapter 15. If your agent is not looking and asking for this information, how can you make certain this agent will understand your company and be able to respond to your needs? If they do not look at all this information, how can they truly help you to improve your organization's Risk Profile and ultimately reduce your overall insurance premiums and total cost of risk? And, if they do not look at all this information, how do you know if they even designed the right retention or insurance program for you?

I mentioned in the previous chapter why the insurance purchasing process is broken. Agents jump in at step four of a five-step program, hoping to place a policy and get a commission doing exactly what they ask, i.e. "Can we quote your insurance?". Hope and quoting are not sound risk management strategies.

Although they say they are going to get you the best rates, they are doing so based on the normal information you provide. By taking the time to go through the entire cycle, you will be rewarded. You will achieve outstanding results similar to our client's results.

Another way to look at the Risk Profile Improvement Process, or the Risk Management Cycle, is to look at large companies. Large box stores, retail chains, multinational manufacturers, banks, and other nationwide companies have an individual that wears only the Risk Management hat. They have a Risk Manager or a CRO (Chief Risk Officer) on staff. They and their team focus 24/7/365 on identifying, managing, controlling and putting programs in place to address risk.

These large multinational companies have the same exposures as your business, just more of them. They also have to hire, manage, keep safe and potentially even fire employees. They have an entire department staffed and at their disposal to help with those processes. Still, most businesses do not have the resources to have a full-blown Risk Manager or Risk Officer on their payroll. This is why it is important that somebody wears that hat for your organization, whether it is you or someone outside your firm, someone who helps you go through the process of identification, analysis, control, transfer and implementation and risk review and refinement. By ultimately focusing on your risks, you will be able to drive down your premiums.

A Word of Caution!

When you are going through this process, do not bite off more than you can chew. The whole idea is to have continual small improvement. The Japanese refer to continual small improvement as *Kiazen*. Strive to improve your risk just half a percent or one percent each month. This may not sound like a large amount, but over time, you will accomplish huge improvements and results. I have met with organizations that attempted to implement too many programs all at once. The long and overwhelming employee training for a large number of new programs leads to confusion, and frequently leads to an increase in the very injuries they were trying to prevent.

After you conduct your risk assessment and you have measured and prioritized your risks, you now want to start picking them off one at a time. Some of these risks you may be able to tackle as a group and some you may have to address individually. You just need to complete them one by one by picking away at the prioritized list of risks and putting your processes in place.

Example

I was referred to an organization by their CPA as he believed his client's costs were out of control when it came to their insurance. The CPA could see the impact the higher premiums had on the financials. However, he did not have a good reference to determine why the premiums were climbing faster than his client was growing. The CPA astutely saw that an analysis was necessary to determine the cause.

We met with the business owner about mid-year during their policy period. When we sat down with this business owner, we found that they would obtain quotes every year. They showed us all of the quotes they received for eight straight years. Despite receiving multiple quotes where the premiums were exponentially increasing each year, the owner believed that the insurance company they were insured by was "the best company for them." While reviewing the quotes, we quickly saw their experience modifier had been climbing the past four years, and the rate the insurance company was using was higher than average. Therefore, it was easy to see that their Risk Profile was deteriorating in the eyes of the insurance companies.

We conducted our Risk Management and HR Assessment to identify what risks and issues they were facing. During this assessment, we identified a number of issues and started eliminating some of the larger ones. We were able to do this very quickly as several were related. What you may find interesting was that we were able to have conversations with several of the insurance companies that had quoted them in the past but were always higher in premium. We asked these insurance companies, based on their perception of risk, what programs or processes they would like to see put in place prior to renewal so that they would be able to give additional consideration when they were rating the insurance next year.

A few of the insurance companies had identified some of the same risks that we had identified. With this company, they had a very large fleet of heavy delivery trucks that were having a significant number of motor vehicle accidents. When reviewing it, we could see that the company's driver selection eligibility program was not utilizing best practices. The company did not qualify, or screen, their drivers so there were a significant number of drivers who had poor driving records. The company only pulled motor vehicle reports to see if they had a valid license. From a *"Perception of additional potential risks and claims"* the number of poor driving records led the underwriters to believe that the company drivers would continue having accidents. Thus, the insurance companies wanted to charge them higher rates.

Working with the employer, we put in place a robust driver selection and eligibility program. We implemented and conducted employee training for a fleet safety program. The employer was even willing to put in place a relatively inexpensive vehicle monitoring system through the tracking of the company-provided hands-free cell phones. This enables employers to know their vehicles' location and speed, as well as where and how long they are stopped. The program also identifies if a vehicle is driving more than five miles per hour over the speed limit and alerts the operations manager.

We also instituted a defensive driving course with additional training in safe driving. Even though some satisfactory programs were in place, they really were not up to best practices.

We placed all the risks we identified, measured and prioritized, on an implementation schedule. Following conversations with the insurance companies, we reprioritized a couple of the risks to make the insurance companies more comfortable with the overall risk of the company.

By simply addressing the fleet issues first, we were able to make this company more attractive to the insurance companies and obtain quotes on their behalf to reduce their auto premium by almost $81,000. The quote they accepted was about $114,000 less than the quote the same insurance company unsuccessfully provided the prior year.

Even though we are discussing vehicles here, looking at their workers' compensation loss runs, you could see that a number of their workers' compensation claims also came from their drivers. Injuries from loading and unloading, as well as motor vehicle accidents were a big concern to the insurance companies.

By addressing the vehicle issues, we also made this company more attractive to the workers' compensation insurance company and enabled the underwriter to justify a 23% lower quote than the year before. This resulted in more than $93,000 in savings over the previous year's policy. This reduction was even more important to this employer as their experience modifier was actually increasing due to their past claims history.

By installing the Risk Profile Improvement Process after identifying these risks through Risk Management and HR Assessment, we were able to reduce insurance costs in less than six months by just over $174,000.

Summarizing this example to demonstrate my premium theorem:

Your claim costs over 5 years	+	Perception of additional potential risks and claims	−	Perception of how much you improved your risk and addressed claims over the past year(s)	=	**Your Risk Profile and Premium**

Claim Costs – The insurance companies had paid (including reserves) $547,000 in wages and medical costs for workers' compensation injuries over five years, as well as almost $228,000 in vehicle accidents.

Plus (+) Potential Injury Perception – Due to past claims history and prior poor motor vehicle reports of the drivers, the underwriters were concerned that there would be a catastrophic vehicle accident leading to a $1 million or even greater lawsuit. They were also concerned about the likelihood of an employee being injured in an accident, or from a serious back or shoulder injury from loading or unloading that would end up lasting years or even go into litigation.

Minus (-) the Improvements – Underwriters believe in implementation of better driver screening including removal of the poor drivers; the fleet safety program; defensive driving training; the enhanced training on loading and unloading; and improving their return-to-work controls.

Equaled = An Improved Risk Profile and a 24% reduction in premium. The underwriter believed that the improvements made more than compensated for any potential risks the underwriter perceived, enabling the underwriter to underwrite to a 35% loss ratio instead of a 25% loss ratio. The dollar amount of the losses did not change; only the perception of the risk that led the underwriter to the comfort level enabling a premium reduction.

You must be able to not just say you made these improvements; you need to be able to tangibly show and demonstrate that the changes were made, and that the changes were meaningful. It is obvious from this example; small changes can have a huge effect. Since then, we have installed additional programs based on the risks identified resulting in premium reduction the following year of an additional $78,000.

Focusing on all stages of the risk management cycle: identify, prioritize and mitigate risks; created a feeding frenzy in the insurance marketplace for this insurance program. You, too, can achieve similar results by going through the entire Risk Management Process with your organization.

In this business owner's case, after a few years of being able to demonstrate that they can better control their risk, prevent claims from occurring, and improve how claims are managed to mitigate their financial costs, it made financial and actuarial sense for the business owner to look into a group captive.

So, I ask again, what is your *Risk Profile*?

———————

Getting the Right People on the Bus

In his best-selling book *Good to Great*, Jim Collins talked about how having the right people in the right seats on your business' bus is the best way to achieve success.

The perfect hand in poker is the Royal Flush. To build a winning hand, you sometimes have to discard poor cards and draw better cards to help your odds of winning. As a business leader your business plays with the cards, or employees that you have. On occasion, you have to discard poor performing employees. But imagine rather than randomly drawing from the deck, if you could pick the perfect cards (employees) you want at the outset?

However, having the perfect cards, or employees, is not enough. Think of it this way, every professional sports team is stacked with talent, but just because you have the best players does not necessarily make you the best team. Your team needs to draft or sign (a.k.a. hire) good talent. That talent then needs to be trained, managed, and practice together; and then be guided and lead by a good coach and coaching staff. That is how you get the most out of your players. Getting all those players to work together makes the best team with the best odds of winning a championship.

When it comes to improving your results, the better you are at hiring and managing your employees (building your hand), the greater the insurance company will like you as a risk. Safety professionals know that over 90% of all claims come from employee actions, so how you hire and manage them is highly critical. So critical, that this topic has spread over three chapters: *Chapter 12 Getting the Right People On The Bus* (hiring and the initial orientation period), *Chapter 13 Improving Your Safety Culture* (developing ongoing behavior based safety/management), *Chapter 14 Effective Claims Management* (improving claims management and return-to-work results).

What I have discovered is that employee problems begin at hire, whether it is from injuries, accidents, or poor performance. Ask yourself: If you were to start all over from scratch in hiring employees to fill all of the positions in your company, would you hire the same employees? Hire the same way you do today? Or would you hire differently?

I understand the potential employee pond is smaller, but that just means you have to use better bait, so to speak, and you need to make sure you are attracting the right "fish," or in this case, the right employee. I know some business leaders might say that they will never be able to hire anybody if they followed everything outlined, but simply ask yourself, "Why are you going to hire a potential problem and pay the costs of hiring them, or replacing them when they do not work out, or paying the cost of higher premiums when they injure themselves?". The cost of hiring the wrong person almost always exceeds the cost of hiring in general.

When it comes to hiring, you may want to begin with the end in mind. You should have the goal of hiring injury-free and productive employees and work backwards to determine what you need to do in order to accomplish this. You can then create the steps and processes necessary to achieve this outcome.

The ideal productive and safe employee would have the skills, education, focus and attitude to be able to complete their job with high efficiency and to do it safely. Productive employees are going to understand specific job duties that they are responsible for and be willing to accomplish them without constant supervision. They know how to conduct all of their required tasks, how to complete them safely and efficiently, and are willing and able to discuss with their supervisor other ways to improve their performance. Constant improvement is in their DNA.

These requirements may be a lot to ask for. Each position in your company may have different nuances that require adjusting what was just spelled out, but I believe you get the point.

To determine what skills and education you need to hire for a specific job, you must understand everything that the position or job requires. Therefore, detailed and written job descriptions are a must. Job descriptions should comprise the following:

- Essential job functions and responsibilities
- Any non-essential functions
- Success factors and job competencies
- Physical demands and requirements
- Performance standards, including skills and education requirements.

However, do not forget to determine the attitude of the employee you want to have in that position. Do you need a self-starter, someone who is outgoing and personable, or someone that is task oriented, or perhaps a facilitator that will want to help your customers?

When you fill this position, you will know exactly what your requirements are and you will be able to conduct tests to determine if a potential employee has the ability and is physically able to complete the job without getting injured. Do not forget the attitude check. You will know what skill sets are required for the job, as well as education. Hire the right skills, attitude and education, and training then becomes easier.

Finding the perfect candidate may seem impossible. However, the job description provides your blueprint for hiring, and then you can build that employee by filling any gaps. So hire first for the attitude (this is the best way to avoid problematic and drama-creating employees), then the physical requirements of the job, and then determine if the employee has the potential and desire to be trained. This way, you can train employees to achieve the required skills.

Attitude Requirements

Attitude could, and most likely should, be the most important requirement. Too often I see employers hire for skill first, but if the employee has a bad attitude they end up creating significant issues and drama within your organization. These employees also tend to become claim problems in the future. If you must have certain skills, look at all candidates that have something close to your minimum skill needs. Hire them based on attitude and train for any gaps.

To recap the job requirements: attitude; tasks, education and skills to accomplish the job; and physical requirement. Now that you have these defined, you can then determine and test your candidates to select the best person for your organization.

There is a multitude of predictive personality or attitude, testing programs available. Some give you the ability to conduct personality tests on current employees so you can determine what personality type your best employees at different positions may be. This will then give you some insight as to what personality type may be best suited for a certain position.

Some of the better testing systems will allow you to test your whole organization and give you a baseline of your overall culture. This allows you to better choose personalities to fit within your organization.

Most offer a nominal paid subscription program so you can test as many candidates as you want. So, in other words, test all candidates and do not just rely on your gut feelings. Many candidates can give you a great first impression that may be masking issues that will crop up later. These tests are designed to uncover those issues.

Education Requirements

It is important to verify your applicant's education and degree from the university, college, trade school, or online school that they graduated from. Verifying their degree through an education background check helps you validate their resume or application. This is necessary because it is possible for a person to embellish their resume. I have seen people actually change their degree to what they perceive to be a better fit for the job, or state that they completed their degree when they either did not complete it or were in the midst of completing it.

Skill Requirements

You must skill test at your facility or jobsite. Request your applicant to complete tasks with the tools, equipment or machines they will work with in their position. This will give you firsthand knowledge as to how well they know what needs to be done, but also if they are conducting the job properly and safely.

Just because they worked as a machinist for three years does not mean they really understand how to operate your equipment. You may want to see if they are capable of performing the functions on a test part in your facility. If you are in the construction world, are they able to discuss with you what specific steps they would have to accomplish to complete the task, or the necessary steps to operate equipment safely?

You have a vast choice of companies that provide online testing for technology or computer intensive positions. You want to make certain that any tests performed are done in your presence. When an applicant takes a test at home, at times they are not taken by the actual candidate, but by one who is more skilled than the prospective employee.

If you do not test the person you are hiring, you may believe you are getting a competent person, or even a "superstar," and you actually hired someone who may need significant training and education to complete the tasks of the job. Not knowing you have hired an undertrained employee, and not training to fill skills and education gaps, will most likely lead to having a "poor performer" or "problematic" employee. This perception develops because it takes the employee much longer to complete tasks as compared to others. More importantly, they may miss critical deadlines, respond slowly, and upset customers.

Physical Requirements

Many employers have hired an employee who quickly becomes 'injured,' but that injury seems to be more a case of a pre-existing condition being aggravated than a new injury. Either way, the employer is not happy when they have to pay for that employee's injury. The only way to prevent 'hiring an injury' is to find out if such a condition exists. However, you cannot ask an employee or potential new employee, such a question.

Due to HIPAA (Health Insurance Portability and Accountability Act), only a doctor can ask a prospective employee about specific medical conditions. Therefore, it is best to work with medical professionals when screening prospective employees. The doctor can determine whether or not the candidate can physically complete the required tasks of the job, or if they need accommodations to do so. The accommodations are important because they address the Americans with Disabilities Act, and whether you are able to accommodate a restriction or not due to the physical requirements of a specific job.

As you can see, it is very important that you determine and write out in detail your specific physical requirements in the job description. If you cannot accurately determine the specific physical requirements of the job, reach out to your local physical therapist. They can come to your facility or job site, observe the jobs, go through the motions required, and determine the actual pounds needed to be lifted, the range of motions needed, etc.

Once you have spelled out the specific requirements, conduct a post-offer, pre-employment physical, including a functional capacity screening. Many physical therapists will gladly assist in establishing the physical requirements of the job for you at no fee. You may then use them to conduct your prospective employee's physical tests to best determine if they can do the essential functions of the job. Testing, if you decide to use it, must be performed for all potential candidates for the job. For example, if you use physical tests for applicants for a carpenter's position, all applicants must be tested. You cannot limit testing to only those candidates you believe pose a risk. You will have to pay the physical therapists to conduct the screening tests, but the tests are nominal compared to how much an injury from a "pre-existing condition" can cost you in increased workers' compensation premiums.

You may also want to have a company doctor, ideally an occupational medicine doctor, conduct the employee physicals. By establishing a "go to" doctor who has seen and understands your business and knows what the various jobs requirements are, you can be certain the doctor is watching out for your company and is less likely to "approve" a person that physically cannot perform the job even with an accommodation. This would be the same doctor you want to send injured employees to in order to make certain you have a doctor that will help you bring the employee back to work as quickly as possible.

If the job requires the employee to routinely lift fifty-pound bags, they should be able to do this without pre-existing conditions. A doctor can look at the applicant for scars on the back, knees, elbows, shoulders, etc., and ask questions to determine if a prior medical condition would affect the applicant's ability to do the job. A doctor's office may be able to simulate minor lifting, but the physical therapist can actually put the prospective employee through a much more diverse series of tests. They can determine if the prospective employee is straining to lift the sack, is favoring a leg, or has some other reason they are not able to complete the physical requirements of the job. A doctor may also be able to describe any accommodation necessary to allow the prospective employee to complete the job. The accommodation can then be reviewed for reasonableness.

Another benefit of conducting the pre-employment functional capacity testing is you may have an employee who can do the job, but only has 90% range of motion in their shoulder. If in the future the employee injures that shoulder, workers' compensation would normally pay benefits to an injured employee's shoulder recovered to 100%, or compensate them if recovery fell short of 100%. By having the pre-employment testing done and recorded, you have documentation the employee had only 90% use of the shoulder and therefore a full recovery is only 90%, and not 100%. This will save you considerable amounts of future premium from the additional claim costs.

Keep in mind, however, that rejecting an applicant because they have prior injuries or need a reasonable accommodation, can result in a discrimination lawsuit. Testing should be done to confirm whether the applicant can perform the essential functions of a job with or without reasonable accommodation. Testing should never be used to eliminate a candidate based on the belief that the prospective employee represents a greater workers' compensation risk.

Application, Interview and Pre-Employment Testing

You are ready to set up your application and interview process now that you know who you need to hire, and what and how you will test for it.

You can conduct the normal reference checks before you offer someone a job. However, before you are able to do any background checks, education and employment verifications, credit checks, personality and skills testing, medical, drug or physical testing, you must make a conditional offer of employment to the candidate. This written offer would be contingent upon the outcomes of the tests that you are going to have them undergo, such as the drug or physical tests, and any consumer reports you are going to review.

For you to be able to conduct any tests and screenings, including reference checks or employment and education verifications, you must have the prospective employee's written authorization. The application or application packet must spell out to the candidate that by signing the release they authorize you to conduct medical and drug testing; obtain employment information, background information such as motor vehicle reports, credit reports, criminal background checks, education, licenses, and basically anything else necessary for that job to be properly done. Authorizations should be separate from the application to ensure that the applicant knowingly allows the searches to be conducted. Medical testing, including drug testing, authorizations must be HIPAA compliant and should not be part of the consumer report or criminal background check authorization.

The human resource attorney for East Coast Risk Management, an organization that I have frequently worked with, offered an additional or alternative method of assessing a candidate's propensity for risk assumption or aversion that is based on psychological reasoning. She stated, "It is my opinion that a motor vehicle report's purpose is two-fold; to ensure a candidate has the ability to legally operate a motor vehicle and that his/her driving record is acceptable for insurance purposes and, secondly, to highlight or indicate a candidate's potential for performing intentionally negligent and reckless acts. In my experience, a candidate who has several moving violations and/or traffic citations or perhaps multiple violations/citations for the same or similar act are generally a higher risk employee for improper employment acts and/or workplace accidents and injuries including vehicle operation regardless of vehicle ownership." Further she stated, "This theory is applicable to all levels of employment or job categories in any industry and to all employers alike."

Once you have described this to the candidate in the application, and provided them with the detailed job description with essential functions and physical requirements of the job, you may legally ask the employee if they are able to perform all essential tasks necessary to perform the job duties. You cannot, however, ask if they have a specific medical condition that would prevent them from doing the job. You are simply asking if they are able to do the job as outlined. You could even ask them to demonstrate how they would lift that fifty-pound sack, by actually lifting it, or by lifting it with a reasonable accommodation. Then you would be able to see if they demonstrate proper lifting techniques. As long as it is material to the job, is in the written job description, and you do this for all applicants, you are not discriminating. You cannot decide whether or not they are medically able to do the job. This would be up to the doctor.

Have your interview questions lined up in advance -- do not "wing it." Some of the best questions to ask are how someone would respond to real world examples of situations your employees have experienced in the past. This can give you some insight as to how they would respond and what their skill sets may actually be.

You want everybody who is hired by your organization to go through this entire process. You cannot take shortcuts. You cannot discriminate. Everyone must go through the same process. You may also want to conduct personality or education testing. All testing, however, must be job-related.

During the interview process you want to introduce what your corporate culture is, especially in terms of safety, work ethic, personal responsibility, etc. This lays the ground work to clearer expectations that will be spelled out when they go through your initial orientation.

Company Culture, Safety and Orientation

Begin by introducing this employee through an orientation program. This orientation should not just be about the history of your company, but much more.

Indoctrinate your employee into your safety culture immediately. Safety begins at hire, so your orientation also needs to start with and continually emphasize safety. OSHA does require you to provide certain training to a new employee before they actually start, such as hazard communication, but this process goes beyond that. Your new employee must understand the culture of your organization in order to do their job not only safely, but productively. They need to understand that you have a "zero-injury culture," that no job is important enough to lose life or limb, and that accidents do not "just happen." The orientation needs to convey that the employee is responsible for themselves and for their team, to make sure everyone is working safely and in a safe environment.

I contend that immediately after the required initial employment paperwork, such as completing the Employment Eligibility Verification Form I-9, that you should conduct the new employee's safety orientation. Your employees need to go through appropriate safety training before they even set foot on the job. This will elevate, as the main priority. the goal of working efficiently and safely.

Many times we see employers make the mistake of waiting for the next safety meeting or the next safety training session to educate the new employee. This can be a month, two months, even six months away, depending on how often they go through this process. And that is totally unacceptable.

The orientation should also emphasize the culture of your organization, the employee's expectations, and what you expect them to do and how to do it. Educate them on who to report to, who should be in the chain of command, what should they be striving for and achieving, and how often you will conduct performance reviews with the employee. It should also spell out the process of reporting issues they identify. The culture of safety should be identified in your employee handbook and supported by the employee safety manual and their safety training. When either hiring or orienting your employee to your company, describe to them what their career ladder path could look like. What would be necessary for them to achieve, learn or understand to move up in the organization?

Keep in mind, when you move a good employee up to a new management position, you must also view that position change similar to hiring a new employee. Confirm they are adequately trained, educated and oriented to that position. Many managers fail because they were great at what they previously did, but they are poor leaders or managers in their new position. They could be too heavy-handed, too light-handed, fail to provide adequate feedback to the employee on how they are performing their job, or whatever the case may be. The last thing you want to do is hire from within and fail to train and orient the employee to their new position. This will also lead to a problematic management employee and potentially problematic employees working beneath that supervisor.

Post Orientation

Would you be surprised to know that there is a higher percentage of new employees injured in the first six months compared to those working in the position longer than six months? You would probably also be surprised to know that the turnover ratio of the newest employees tends to be higher than your seasoned employees. Because of these issues, you should change how you manage your employees during and following their "probationary period."

If you read articles on hiring and managing a young employee, you will see the term Pre-Frontal Cortex, which is basically the cause and effect portion of the brain ("If I do this, that will happen"), that has been delayed in development from people early in their mid-teen years to now well into their twenties, because of the way children are being raised today.

An extreme example of this might be the much-publicized December 2013 court case where a Texas judge sentenced then 16-year-old Ethan Couch (who drove drunk and caused a crash, killing four people and injuring two) to 10 years probation and no jail time. His story made national headlines after a witness, a psychologist named G. Dick Miller, claimed Couch was a victim of "affluenza," resulting from being the product of wealthy, privileged parents who never set limits for the boy. Basically, the psychologist tried to make a case for the defense team, saying that how Couch was raised resulted in his not knowing any better, or being able to understand the consequences of his actions, and therefore he was not responsible for the crime he committed.

After understanding that brain development changed, we started to change the process of training new employees for our clients to be longer, as well as increasing the points of communication with the new employee. We focused on reducing the frequency and severity of injuries in newer employees by changing the orientation and mentoring period from normally one or two weeks to three or four weeks, which has yielded not only fewer injuries, but also yielded a higher rate of employee retention. The normal 90-day "probationary period" may not need to change time-wise, but how you engage with the employee throughout those 90 days will need to.

You will want to sit down more frequently with the employee in a group meeting that engages the supervisor, the mentor and employee (the employee's "orientation team"). You should have daily meetings with the employee's orientation team. These short discussions are to communicate that, "These are all the things you're doing well," because newer employees need to be patted on the back routinely, as well as being told, "This is what you need to work on."

The goal during the initial period is to establish good habits while trying to identify any skills or knowledge gaps that may indicate a need for certain training. You also want to reinforce throughout this process that the reason why the company does things a particular way is because through prior efforts it was determined that this is the best and safest way of doing something.

Things often change when you have the mentor step away and the employee work on their own. Younger employees are typically very bright, full of ideas, curious, and have been encouraged by their parents to try new things. Therefore, they are more likely to try things without thinking of the repercussions (see cause and effect above). If you think of the initial mentoring period as crawl before you walk, and have ever raised a child, you know that as soon as they begin to walk, they want to run. This next phase of the employee orientation and training, the walk before they run, is the restraint needed not to discourage them.

The mentor needs to step back and be a remote observer at this point. The employee needs to work on their own without the mentor stepping in frequently, yet still observing. The employee's orientation team still needs to meet daily to discuss not only the good and the bad, but also continue to identify if there are any gaps in skills or knowledge necessary to effectively do the job. If it any point during this process a gap is identified, the employee needs to be pulled back and the necessary training and education needs to again take place so they can continue to be productive.

The main goal of this period is to prevent bad habits before they start. With younger workers, if you are not identifying their skills gap or knowledge gaps and providing the training and education to close those gaps, they will try to creatively figure it out and probably do something wrong or get themselves hurt or damage property/equipment. The quicker you close the employee's skill gap, the quicker they will be safe and productive for you.

The other key concept that you need to convey to the employee at this time is that as they do their work, they should come up with ideas on their own to do their work more quickly or efficiently, and that you are open to their suggestions and their creativity. However, you also need to clearly convey to them that they should never try their idea without first having a discussion with their orientation team and receiving approval to do so. The employee's orientation team is willing to work with them on this idea, but as the orientation team is more experienced, they may bring up some additional questions or concerns that will need to be addressed before trying the process, so it can be done safely.

The one thing that we have found to be most successful, however, is to make certain that the orientation team does not step out of the employee's "world" when working there. As you close the knowledge training and skills gaps, and confirm the employee is working safely and efficiently, you can begin to reduce those short brief meetings from their initial daily sessions to a couple of days per week, then fewer days per month, etc. However, with these younger workers, as well as a worker of any age, you should on at least a quarterly basis communicate to them the positive things that they do and if necessary, identify and communicate things that they need to work on. Frequent communication is the basis of any effective performance management program.

Also, when you start a new employee in their position, or move an employee to a new position, train them for that job. Rather than showing them once or twice how to do something, and then leaving them on their own, you need to have a mentoring program. A mentoring program is where a more experienced employee, one that does things the proper way, is able to monitor and make sure the new employee:

1. Conducts their tasks properly and safely.
2. Does not slip into any bad habits that will be more difficult to break later on.
3. Does not have any skill gaps that need to be addressed.

It is important that the mentor:

1. Works with the new employee for a period of time.
2. Is responsible for monitoring and making sure the employee knows what they are
       doing.
3. Will assess if the employee is conducting the job safely and correctly.
4. Acts as a sounding board for the employee to ask questions as they start to learn their
       position.

The more rapidly you get the employee to the point where they truly understand their job and how to conduct it, and have the necessary skills to perform it, the happier, safer and more productive your employee will be.

After you reach this point, be sure to provide periodic assessments and consistent reviews of their performance. On an ongoing basis, you should identify not only the areas where you can help them improve, but also commend them for the good things they accomplish. Also, look for feedback on how they feel they or the company can improve.

You would be amazed how often your own employees will be able to identify better, safer and more productive ways to accomplish the same task, or have ideas on how the company can grow as a whole. Proper employee management will lead to safer and more productive employees, and your employee's focus on doing what they should be doing will help improve the indicators, or telltale signs, that insurance companies look for when analyzing your company. Therefore, you will see improvement in your Fleet & Driver Safety, Quality Control, Housekeeping, Policies & Procedures, Processes, Facility & Equipment Maintenance, and other areas scored by underwriters.

13

Improving Your Safety Culture

Even in the captive world, the reinsurance companies will want to make sure that you have robust policies and procedures in place when it comes to quality control, fire safety, and employee safety. They are certainly going to inspect your operation, not only to see what programs you have in place, but if those programs are active and enforced. They will be looking for the following programs:

- Personal Protective Equipment
- Machine Guarding
- Equipment Maintenance
- Lock-Out/Tag-Out
- Hot Work Permit
- Lifting/Material Handling
- NOISE/Hearing Conservation
- Confined Space Entry
- Hazard Communications / Material Safety Data Sheets (Right to know)
- Other safety requirements based on your business

However, being OSHA compliant does not mean you have a safe and productive workforce. A safety culture is driven from the top down as well as from the bottom up. How apparent the *effectiveness* of these programs is when the captive safety person inspects them is the key.

So why should safety be a main focus of your company?

When Paul O'Neill first became CEO of Alcoa, everybody expected he would be conducting expansion or undertaking acquisitions in order to boost shareholder value. But much to everyone's surprise, the first thing he actually did was improve an already significantly better than average safety program. He said the reason was that safety affects every employee in the company, and he believed the most productive way of doing something is also the safest way of doing something. As a result, he drove the company to extremely high levels of productivity and profitability. I highly recommend you read the book, *Power of Habit* by Charles Duhigg, particularly chapter four, which highlights the safety efforts put forth by Paul O'Neill.

O'Neill did this because he wanted to change the culture of the organization; to make it a better-performing organization. He made safety everyone's responsibility, not just the loss control people on staff. Alcoa's productivity soared and injuries were dramatically reduced. O'Neill proved safety and productivity can work in harmony and, in fact, safer practices *can* lead to better production and profit. Once again, O'Neill drove home the idea by bringing his company to extremely high levels of productivity and profitability, and by doing so clearly demonstrated that **the best and most productive way of doing something is also the safest way.**

The problem is many business leaders are incorrectly focused on productivity first and "safety training" second, and only then to the extent of meeting OSHA compliance. Let us give OSHA credit, as they have done a great job over the years of reducing injuries and creating safer work environments. However, the focus has mainly been on the physical conditions and making sure required training is done. One thing is for certain, being OSHA compliant does not mean you are a safe company, and it does not mean the employees will understand and follow your training.

Most training done by companies is necessary and good, but often times it gets lumped in amongst other trainings, or it takes such a long period of time that it gets to the point where the employees' eyes glaze over and they begin to lose focus. For example, I met with an executive of a roofing contractor who said they are a safe company and provide ongoing training to their employees. But when you dig into their safety program you see it only consists of training from a "safety" company that comes in every year and conducts the required training – all in one very, *very* long day. Even worse, a new employee has to wait months for their first training. Yet many employers cannot understand why they pay so much for insurance and cannot get out of the Assigned Risk Pool. They argue that the insurance companies are way too picky when they do an inspection. However, it is often insurance companies who cite unsafe work environments and poor training as the reason not to provide a quote.

There are employers who tell me everything that occurred was an accident and no one could have prevented it from happening. However, my years of experience tell me that the number of actual accidents is few and far between. These employers are making excuses for their poor practices. Case in point, DuPont conducted a study of over 40,000 injuries. They broke their findings into three categories of injury causes: unsafe conditions or environment; unsafe employee action; and accidents where no cause could be determined. What they discovered was that over 80% of all injuries come from unsafe employee actions. Unsafe conditions attributed to 19% of the injuries, and accidents were less than 1% of all injuries.

I contend the focus on OSHA compliance and conducting safety training is good, but it is not attacking the heart of why most injuries occur. In too many injuries an employee says they tripped over this or fell over that or were struck by this. But many times it is because an employee ignored the current situation and did not correct something that became an unsafe condition or environment, or the employer and employees ignored general housekeeping. Based on this, if employees eliminated unsafe conditions that they themselves may have created, you could safely assume that over 90%, or possibly all 99% (leaving only the 1% that are "true" accidents), of injuries could be preventable. Therefore, it really comes down to employee behavior.

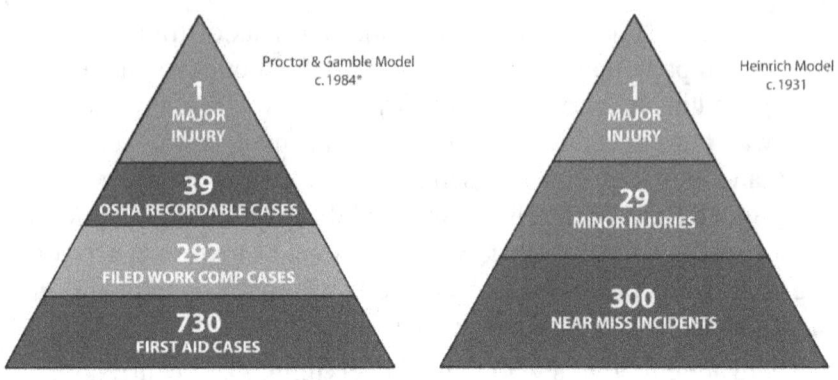

Insurance companies and loss control professionals predominately follow two models: The Heinrich Model, where for every 300 near misses there creates 29 minor injuries and one major injury; or the Procter & Gamble Model, where 730 first aid cases becomes 292 filed workers' compensation cases leading to 39 OSHA recordable cases, all ending with one major injury. Both of these models focus on understanding what has occurred in the past and then trying to correct that situation so, hopefully, it will not happen again. They look to engineer a solution, or try to throw some training at it so the employees will not do it again. As you can see, it is a very reactive model. It also focuses too much on the physical conditions and what has already happened, while failing to identify something new that could happen in the future.

Very early in my career, while working with my dad in our family insurance agency, I learned the traditional safety models did not work. I remember vividly the eerie silence instead of the deafening noise usually heard when I arrived at a very large manufacturing plant. The rescue crews were bringing out an employee who had been killed repairing a machine that had just stopped working. He had turned off the circuit breaker to the machine and was replacing a drive belt inside it when a co-worker accidentally turned the circuit back on when trying to restore power to another machine.

To this day, I still wonder exactly why the deceased employee did not take the time to install the circuit breaker lock that was in his tool bag, per the manufacturer's lock-out/tag-out program he was trained on. I can only speculate that the employee did not install the circuit breaker lock because replacing the drive belt takes less than 10 minutes, and he thought nothing would occur in such a short period of time.

This employee was a husband and father of two very young children. Yes, workers' compensation paid a benefit to the employee's spouse. However, what did it really do for the family? I learned at this point that even one injury can be one too many. I learned that focusing on just providing insurance was not enough. This event caused me to begin to focus more on reducing risks and affecting employee behavior, and not simply focusing on general safety and our client's insurance policies.

The best solution to improving safety, quality and productivity is a behavior-based program approach. It is creating a proactive approach. It simply focuses on the fact that the most productive way of doing something is the safest way. It focuses on the entire employee from head to toe, building a culture, an attitude, and desired employee behavior. Doing so prevents incidents from occurring and encourages an employee to identify those potential hazards, or problems, before they occur, as well as convey potentially better ways of doing things that could be, not only safer, but more productive. In other words, getting the employee to take that second or two to think to himself, "Should I let my hand go so close to a blade? Should I put the guard back on? Should I reach into the machine this way and now? Should I move the patient this way? Should we be installing this equipment a different way? Is there a better way of doing this?".

Interestingly, Procter & Gamble has added behavior to the base of their pyramid. So, clearly behavior-based safety is the antidote to address most injuries. Company management must adopt a mindset and policy of zero injuries and that all accidents are preventable.

The goal of behavior-based management is to encourage every employee to think and take that one second to say, "If I do this, in this fashion, could I get hurt or cause damage to something?". It is also about employees recognizing and speaking out about a co-worker or a supervisor who is not doing something safely or creating a situation that is potentially dangerous. It is also about, as mentioned before, promoting a culture for employees to speak up about issues and potential solutions to improve productivity and safety.

Changing the culture and implementing a robust behavior-based program is a marathon, not a sprint. This is not something you are going to introduce in one meeting and everything is all set. It is going to take time.

The Behavior Based Model

So you ask: "What do we need to do to establish and maintain a behavior-based management system?" Well, first, you need to define the mission and objectives of your program. Is it an organization-wide strategic plan for safety? Second, establish how you will measure and benchmark the behaviors of the employees and how you will gauge overall improvement. Third, establish accountability for behaviors and peer review processes. And four, establish what all levels of the organization will be responsible for.

1 – The Mission Statement

Senior leadership, owners and executives must be involved. This must be communicated downwards through the organization and must be delivered to stress that safety over just productivity is the priority. Doing something safely does not mean doing something slow. But doing something too fast can certainly mean doing something unsafely. Ultimately, those that will be held accountable should be involved in setting deeper objectives so they understand what needs to be done.

2 – Benchmarking.

If you do not measure and record, you cannot determine if you are achieving improvement. Items you may want to record and benchmark might include OSHA recordable and DART rates (Days Away, Restricted Duty, or Transitional Duty), so you can compare them to other peer organizations. You should also include items such as near misses and observed unsafe actions that did not result in an injury or property damage, but were "near misses." Keep in mind that OSHA recordable, DART and near misses should all have specific numeric goals established that reduce over time. This way you can determine the success of your program.

You also want to track items that are deficient, such as not meeting quality controls, or client/patient complaints.

However, reporting by peers or supervisors of observed improper actions should not have specific numeric goals of being reduced over time. This may sound contradictory, but we have seen supervisors not record such incidents as they were afraid that they may be reprimanded, lose their job or a bonus, because they are not observing fewer unsafe actions. Remember, the goal is to prevent the injury or poor-quality work, not just to make the paperwork look good. Therefore, any and all improper actions need reporting, even if no injuries or close calls occur, so that potential problem areas or employees can be addressed before something serious occurs.

Senior management must track and measure various components to hold the supervisors accountable. Yes, even the executives of the organization must monitor those below them to establish the supervisor is doing his or her job. Nothing undoes a safety program quicker than a supervisor who is only focused on productivity with no regard for safety.

Establish a line of communication for feedback from bottom to top. In other words, if an employee feels their supervisor is ignoring a situation that has been brought to their attention, they must feel safe that they can go above their supervisor without fear of repercussions and know who they can go to in such a circumstance.

3 – Establishing accountability and a Peer Review Process

This starts with the owners, executives or CEO reviewing senior management; senior management reviewing supervisors; and supervisors reviewing workers. There should also be a peer review process. This process should include a co-worker acting as the safety person of the day, or it could be a long-time employee responsible for observing the operations of their co-workers because a supervisor may not always be present or even fully aware of all the exposures associated with doing a job.

Basically, you must be able to create a checklist of unsafe/improper behaviors and proper behaviors for supervisors and peer observers to use. Measuring and recording is the key to this process. You will need ongoing training for observers so they can learn from each other, as well from the outside. More importantly, as your team learns these items and actions, corrections must be recorded in the training manual. This allows training of observer's company-wide as well as new observers who can be trained to monitor their co-workers.

4 – Responsibility

In establishing organizational responsibility levels, please understand it is a two-way street up and down the organization. Those below must feel free to "go up the ladder," even several rungs, to ensure key issues and situations are addressed. All goals and actions should be result-oriented. Everything requires reporting and measuring otherwise it ends up meaningless and without consequences. All of this will ultimately improve behavior.

Subsets of the levels of accountability involve personal, team, and organizational accountability:

- *Personal*

You must empower and make each employee responsible for their own actions.

- *Team*

There is shared accountability for the performance of a work group or team through the use of peer review.

- *Organizational*

There is internal accountability, not only up and down the chain, but also externally to those who are working at a job site, client facilities or homes, etc. The actions of others that could put your employees in harm's way affect your property, and vice versa. From an accountability standpoint, you have the obligation to make certain you make others aware of an unsafe situation so that your employees are not in harm's way or that work is damaged. And always correct a situation that may be creating unsafe situations for your employees.

As an example of what is necessary when implementing a behavior-based safety program, we will discuss a building material dealer who had a delivery truck show up at 4:30 on a Friday afternoon to drop off an order of kitchen cabinets. All the loading dock spots were full of trucks being packed, or already packed up, for next-day deliveries. The driver wanted to leave as quickly as possible. He went to the supervisor and said, "Hey, I need to get going. Can you get one of your employees to help unload the truck?". The supervisor sent one of the employees out into the yard to start unloading the truck. In the course of unloading the truck and removing the cabinets, the employee fell off the back of the truck shattering his elbow.

This was not a safe environment for the employee, but the driver, supervisor and even the employee himself, were put in harm's way because they were focused on getting the truck out as quickly as possible instead of pulling the truck into the loading dock. They could have moved one of the fully loaded trucks, thereby allowing the truck to come in and get unloaded safely. Moving a loaded truck would have probably taken less than five minutes, and actually would have shortened the amount of time needed to unload the truck, in the middle of the yard, thereby getting the impatient driver home quicker. This incident could have been prevented by the supervisor saying "no" to the driver. He could have done so by simply stating they were not allowed to unload a truck out in the yard and it would only take a couple of minutes to get a truck moved so the driver could pull in.

The result is an employee who will forever have problems with his elbow, and an employer whose experience modifier increased because of the over $100,000 in medical costs associated with rebuilding and repairing the elbow. This resulted in over $130,000 in additional premium over the impact life of the claim on the modifier. This occurred because the supervisor put perceived productivity ahead of safety. So the additional cost of possibly having an employee work an extra 5-10 minutes of overtime was miniscule in comparison to the additional costs associated with this injury.

So, what occurred? From an employer's standpoint, the employer correctly suspended the supervisor without pay for two weeks to reinforce to all his employees and supervisors that management will not tolerate unsafe actions or short cuts. To have your message "heard" by your employees, you must reinforce your message with consequences.

As you can see, the goal of every organization is not just to be OSHA compliant, but to actually create a safer, more productivity-oriented culture, much like Paul O'Neill did at Alcoa.

Effective Claims Management

In the traditional insurance world, I usually have a business leader ask me, "Why do I have to bring an injured employee back to work and pay them for not doing what I need them to do? Isn't that why I have workers' compensation insurance?". The question usually stems from the concept of business leaders that they buy workers' compensation to pay the claim, and paying an employee to not do their job seems counterproductive and therefore costs them additional money. Being that you are considering captives, you clearly understand you are paying for your own employees' injuries.

Side bar - If for some reason, you are still thinking that you should buy insurance from a captive because it is cheaper insurance, and that let the captive and reinsurer pay the claim, a captive might not be the right option for you. In this case, you may want to read *Stop Being Frustrated & Overcharged* to have a better understanding as to how workers' compensation works and how the insurance industry gets you to repay them for your employee injuries, *plus interest. Remember, insurance companies are For Profit companies.*

Aggressively managing injuries by bringing injured employees back to work quickly, even into a different role in your company, is critical as it affects your employee, your claim costs, your potential underwriting profits, and your premium. Yes, even in a captive. Remember, your loss fund is calculated based on your own history, and then fees are added to it for expenses including charges for claims handling and reinsurance. Therefore, the larger your claims are, the larger your loss fund will be, and therefore the larger your expense fees will be.

To have the best opportunity for receiving larger underwriting profits back from your captive, as well as keeping your actuarially calculated loss funds as low as possible, your first line of defense is to have in place a very detailed and robust accident/incident investigation program, which will determine the root cause and potential corrective action that needs to take place. When done correctly, an accident investigation program can help prevent fraud or exaggerated injuries. By having the proper documentation, including witness statements and those from the employee and the supervisor, it will help keep the employee from being able to change their story or create a fraudulent injury. However, keep in mind that you need to do an investigation as to whether or not the employee wants to claim an injury. Too many times we hear an employee say, "I'll just shake it off," only to file a claim a few days later, when an investigation is less effective. We will dig into accident investigations at the end of this chapter.

Your second line of defense is having a relationship with a medical clinic that understands and manages workers' compensation injuries. You want a doctor that understands what you do, how you do it, and how you operate. If the doctor does not know you and you do not know him, then that doctor is going to listen to the injured employee say, "I lift 50 to 100 pounds all day and I can't go back to work feeling like this." When in reality, that injured employee may never have to lift more than 10 or 25 pounds in the course of a workday.

A very critical part to the return-to-work process is having a list of jobs descriptions ready for medium, light, and even sedentary type duties. Nobody should sit at home. Why? Simply because you will be paying the employee to sit at home and it will cost you underwriting profits from your captive, so you might as well pay the employee to come to work. Plus, all the medical evidence shows that an employee heals faster and better when being involved at work than they would sitting at home. Therefore, recovery time and claims costs will be reduced significantly if they work in some sort of transitional duty.

Part of this process is having job descriptions for all the various jobs in your company. An employee may not need to be 100% recovered in order to get back to work. Doctors may want a copy of their actual job description as well as any transitional duty jobs being considered. More importantly, having job descriptions also ties into the hiring process that we covered earlier on preventing hiring employees with fraudulent or pre-existing injuries.

Working with a doctor that does not require an employee to return to work is very frustrating for employers who understand the value of an early return-to-work process. Let me also give you a bit of background on why some injury management problems may be occurring, and an understanding as to why injury costs are escalating.

The National Council of Compensation Insurance (NCCI) has been tracking workers' compensation costs for decades. There has been a significant change in how the costs line up. For example, in 1987, medical costs represented 46% of all injury costs, and indemnity (wages) payments were 54%. Shift to 1997, just 10 years later, and medical costs were 53% compared to wages at 47%. In 2007, medical costs went up to a whopping 59% while wages reduced to 41%.

On the surface it could be viewed as a result of companies doing a better job of returning employees to work. But in reality, the amount paid to employees out of work due to an injury is actually up. It is just that the amount spent on medical care is exploding. This is why health insurance premiums are also increasing.

Through all of this, the insurance companies and third-party administrators have been increasing their focus on reducing medical costs, particularly through the reduction of fees to doctors and facilities. The insurance companies even tout the "savings" to their clients as a way of showing where their medical cost containment programs have brought them.

Interestingly enough, at the 2012 NCCI conference in Orlando, Florida, the NCCI announced that these fee reductions have had little impact on curtailing medical costs. Focusing on the medical fees is really not the solution; you need to focus on having the injured employee receive the best treatment as quickly as possible. This includes both the quality of medical treatment the employee receives *and* how the employee is treated by your company.

You need to take charge of the process, because if you do not you are leaving it to the whim of the doctor, the insurance company, perhaps even the employee himself as to when he is fit to return to work.

Business people often rely on the insurance company adjuster for input as to when to bring the employee back to work. This is the issue because insurance companies try to keep their expense costs as low as possible, whereas many adjusters are servicing upwards of 250 or more claims at one time. The "best" insurance companies try to keep their average claims per adjuster at around 100 claims or less, which means they would have more time to focus on managing your claims as compared to an adjuster with over 250 claims. However, if you ask them how many total claims they handle, and how many trainee adjusters they have working on cases, you will find that the seasoned adjusters are still probably handling 150 or more claims. The problem ends up being that your priority—which is your claim—may not necessarily be the priority of that adjuster. You must take control of the process yourself.

Ask yourself: Who are the three most impactful people when it comes to having a better outcome?

- **The Doctor**

    The doctor can understand that an employee being at work recovers quicker than one who is sitting at home. They can understand that not being sedentary is actually good for an employee's healing process. Plus, the loss of a significant social environment at work can weigh heavily on an employee's psyche. Or, they can send the injured employee home.

- **The Employer**

    The employer can be caring. They can bring the employee back to work. They can accommodate any variety of conditions and provide meaningful work, so that the employee feels he is still a valuable member of the team. Or, they can send the employee home.

- **The Employee**

The employee can either be compliant or disruptive. They could follow the suggestions and recommendations of the doctors and try to recover as quickly as possible and return to work. Or, they can become disruptive. They could seek out an attorney. They could exaggerate how serious their condition is to the doctor in order to receive time off from work.

If you look at it, these are the three most important people and organizations that affect an outcome. You may notice the adjuster is missing from this group. Although the adjuster is important, he can only manage and react based on the decisions of the other three.

If the doctor says the employee is to be out of work, then all the adjuster can do is wait for the doctor to release the employee to full or modified duty, or order an independent medical evaluation and fight to bring the employee back sooner. If the employee wants to get an attorney, an adjuster really cannot stop it. When that occurs, they have to go into the mode of settling the claim as quickly as possible to reduce overall costs.

The Doctor

Clearly the doctor wields the pen and is critical in this process. You need to choose, and choose wisely. Some of the questions you need to ask yourself are:

- Are you relying on a doctor that the insurance company provided to you, or one off a discount provider list?
- Do you know who your doctor is when an employee suffers an injury?
- Do you know what experience the doctor has in treating workers' compensation injuries? Keep this in mind: many doctors seek to treat workers' compensation injuries because

it is currently more lucrative from a fee schedule than healthcare. In the past, many doctors ran from it because it was less lucrative.

- What is your doctor's return-to-work philosophy?
- How will the doctor communicate with you and how often?
- What kind of wait times does the doctor have?
- What exactly are the doctor's capabilities? Are they able to remove metals from the eye, provide sutures, and take x-rays, for example? Or will you have to send the employee to an Emergency Room to get these services? Keep in mind when using an Emergency Room that the odds are the medical costs and chances of the employee being taken off work will be much higher.
- Did the doctor come and tour your facility to understand the requirements of the jobs?
- More importantly, does the doctor know what your capabilities are in terms of early return to work?
- Is the doctor related by ownership or contract with secondary facilities such as physical therapy or imaging facilities? In some cases, we have seen higher than average utilization of those facilities. It would not be unexpected for someone, who is looking to offset the fee reductions for each service to increase the overall number of services.
- Does the doctor follow ACOEM (American College of Occupational and Environmental Medicine) standards? Doctors who follow these standards are typically Occupational Medicine doctors who are specifically trained to deal with work-related injuries. By following the ACOEM standards, the doctor has best practices guidelines to follow for each type of injury rather than doing multiple tests that most likely have no bearing on the injury.

You need to create doctor relationships that will work best to bring the employee back to work and provide better employee care. This ultimately leads to better medical outcomes, which leads to less medical costs and far less wage or indemnity costs because the employee is back to work quicker and everyone is ultimately happier in the end.

The Employer

Demonstrate that you care. Statistics show that 70% of employees off work did not hear from their supervisor, a co-worker, or anybody other than the HR or Workers' Comp administrator from the time they were off to the time that they returned. How does this make your employee feel?

Second, you need to find meaningful work for the employee. Ask your managers or supervisors for unfinished projects that need completing. Ask them what they would like to get done if they had more time and more help. You can even create a temporary position, such as Safety Monitor, where you provide observation checklists for the employee to go through the facility or job site to determine if the employees are doing what they are supposed to be doing.

Most importantly, you do not want to pay the employee to sit at home. Yes, it saves you money from the Payback Ratio of your experience modifier, and it does make the insurance company somewhat happy that they are paying out less money, but it will not improve the outcome any more than if they were receiving compensation from your workers' compensation insurance company. I have seen many an injured employee paid to stay home, only to eventually wind up with a very big settlement check.

The overriding fact we see relating to the success of bringing an injured employee back to work is their relationship with their supervisor. If they have a good relationship with the supervisor prior to the injury, they typically will come back to work faster. However, if that relationship is suffering, it may be more difficult. It is critical for you to train your supervisors on the importance of why employees must follow the company's early return-to-work program.

A supervisor's relationship with your injured employees, and how the supervisor communicates, measures the success of your return-to-work program. Supervisors who communicate poorly, have a poor attitude, or do not care, will sink your return-to-work program.

Clearly, you need to provide meaningful work to your employee to get them back as quickly as possible. Make sure the doctor on your team will send them back to work. Even though 24% of injuries result in an employee off work for more than three days, statistics show that it should really only be 10%. The difference is a result of not having an active, successful return-to-work program, not having a doctor who understands your organization, and not communicating your expectations properly with your employee.

As we mentioned, currently 60% of injury costs come from medical costs and 40% from indemnity wages. I contend that by getting the injured employee the right care as quickly as possible, and controlling the wages more and getting the employee back to work as quickly as possible, you will actually reduce your overall medical costs. When an employee wants to stay off work, they have to find more and more reasons to go to the doctor to get permission to stay off work.

If you are still questioning having an employee come back to work on transitional duty, you might be thinking right now, I remember reading that I will have more control of the claims management process with a captive. If I want a nurse case manager – I will get one. If I want surveillance – done. If I do not want a claim paid because I believe it is questionable – not so fast there. Short answer, yes you have more control, but the required state insurance department adjuster still has to follow state laws and cannot deny a claim or stop paying one just because you want to. They will need the necessary documentation showing that an injury did not occur on the job before they can deny it, which is why the robust accident investigation is needed.

Yes, you have control over your claims, however, if you need to rely on the tactics of surveillance or nurse case managers to deal with a claim, most likely you are not in control of that claim, the injured employee is. When the employee is at work you are in control of the claims management process, and when they sit at home, they are.

The Employee

What I have found over time is there are basically two types of employees: good employees and bad employees. However, there are subsets. You have good employees who, no matter what, will always be good. They will come back to work and follow the doctor's instructions. They will never be a problem.

You can have bad employees that will remain bad, no matter how much you and the doctors try. To be honest, if you think you have a bad employee you are much better off getting them out of your organization before they become an injury or claim.

On rare occasions, you can have a bad employee that turns good. Usually, the employee will not turn good after they are injured, but it could happen before they are injured if you appropriately engage them in a corrective process. You can try to change their attitude or whatever the case may be. However, if you cannot turn them around you should probably eliminate them from your organization or, as my one of my friends says, "I am going to help them free up their future."

However, many times we see good employees who turn bad. When I talk to employers about a particular claim, especially a large claim, I hear many times the employer was surprised that this employee took advantage of them.

When drilling down on a claim, we usually find the employee sat at home for a while with no contact from the employer, other than maybe the HR person, and no contact from any of their co-workers. Perhaps they are watching daytime TV with endless ads for workers' compensation attorneys. Much later, after the employee has been sitting there, the insurance company urges the employer to bring the employee back to work. The insurance company wants the employer to start putting pressure on the employee to return to work.

In some cases, the employee has shown up but often been handed meaningless work. When this happens, the employee may view this as harassment (or disrespect) or that the job was given to them as a kind of punishment.

The key is to educate your injured employee on what to expect, and what you expect from them. You need to explain that you care about them, that you expect them to go to the doctor, that you expect them to follow the care plan, and that you want them to have a full recovery first and foremost. Also, explain they will need to return to work because they are a *valued member of your team*. Let them know that if they cannot do their original job, even with some alterations, that you have other key projects they can do that are less physical.

Continually reach out to that employee if they are away from work for more than one day. It might be a co-worker, a supervisor, or even an executive. An injured employee should be everyone's concern, and everyone needs to engage with the employee on an ongoing basis in order to reinforce that you want them to get well quickly, that you miss them, and that you need them back on the team.

Your strongest deterrent from an injured employee lawsuit is that *nobody sues someone they like*. Maintaining a good relationship with your employee is the key.

Accident Investigation

As mentioned before in Workers' Compensation Injury, a robust accident/incident investigation program is your first line of defense when it comes to an employee injury, and the same can be true of any incident. Not only does it help prevent fraud or exaggerated injuries, it also becomes extremely vital in catastrophic cases.

For instance, an incident/accident investigation becomes important when an at-fault driver attempts to blame an auto accident on your driver and is claiming injuries, or an employee is claiming that they were being harassed at work for an extended period of time leaving them with emotional damages, or a consumer is claiming they were injured by your product but was actually using it for a purpose it was not designed for. By having the proper documentation, including the statements from witnesses, the employee, and the supervisor, it helps keep the employee from being able to change their story or create a fraudulent injury.

While participating at the 2016 Pennsylvania School Bus Association Annual Conference, I was fortunate to sit in on another presenter's session where an attorney was speaking about post collision/accident issues and their impact on settlements and judgments. The attorney specialized on defense and investigation of commercial vehicle and construction accident cases. He commented that an accident investigation is critical to your success in court, that it will 'make or break you' when it comes to catastrophic cases. He further commented that too often investigations are done improperly, or done in a manner that the employee was trying to get the investigation over quickly rather than doing the investigation needed, in as much detail as possible. He expressed that the poor investigations he received from his client would yield large settlements or judgments, and this lead him to conduct the accident investigation all over again to try and improve his client's position.

I found a reoccurring theme when I was talking to a workers' compensation defense attorney who stated that over 90% of the cases that they took to court did not have a thorough investigation completed prior to the law firm's involvement. And when working on trying to gather and recreate the investigation usually more than a year later, it was difficult to do so. No wonder why so many times the employee wins.

When it comes to accident investigations, you need to think like a detective trying to solve a case of what, where, why, who and how. Here are the key components to an accident investigation:

- *Employee Statement* – It is critical that you get the employee's statement in writing as soon as possible.

- *Witness Statements* – It is better to get these right away before they start talking to others or the employee involved and their recollection of the event changes. You also want to know what occurred prior to and after the incident. Was the injured employee seen limping into work for example?

- *Supervisor Investigation* – It is best to have the immediate supervisor conduct the incident investigation as they know the employee the best and would pick up on anything out of the ordinary.

- *Safety Committee Investigation* – Yes, you should have your safety committee review the incident to see if there are any pieces missing or if something does not make sense. They may even want the employee to "recreate" or walk through the event with them at the scene.

- *Doctor Report* – It is important to get the cause of injury from the doctor as sometimes what the employee tells the doctor may be different than what they state to their supervisor. Or, maybe the degree or type of injury was not possible with regards to what the employee stated happened.

- *Root Cause* – It is important to clearly understand how and why an incident occurred so that you can defend yourself from a possible lawsuit if you are not negligent, plus you also need to determine what to do to prevent it from happening again.

- *Corrective Action* – Now that you clearly know what occurred, the next step is putting programs or safety practices into place, or alter a machine, so that an injury does not occur the same way in the future.

You might be thinking this is a lot to do, but when it comes to being able to defend yourself, or manage a problematic (or even fraudulent) injury, doing all of these steps will be worth it both financially and emotionally.

Case in point. We had a client of ours that called to report an employee injury to our claims staff. The injured employee reported to work Monday morning. While on the way to the locker room, the employee said he was asked to help get something down of the shelf as he is a rather big, strong guy. While getting it down, he slipped on the ladder and tweaked his knee. The doctor he went to see put him off of work and scheduled him to see an orthopedic surgeon due to tears in the knee.

When the claims person was asking a few additional questions beyond the Employer's Workers' Compensation First Report of Injury Form, something seemed amiss. The client was also concerned and confused about why and how it occurred, so we sent one of our safety professionals to assist the owner and supervisor with the investigation.

Interestingly enough, there was no witness to him on the ladder and the fellow employee that the injured employee said asked for the item stated that he did not ask for it. We also found that the employee did not park in the employee lot nor enter through the main or employee entrances that had surveillance, but came in through a secure fire door that another employee opened for him. In fact, one employee interviewed said he saw the employee limping on way the way into side door. Another employee in a completely different department said that the employee was involved in an event at the local fire hall over the weekend. Looking at the Facebook page of the volunteer fire department showed that they had a studio wrestling fundraiser event.

After the claims and safety team discovered all of this, they contacted the wrestling operation who stated that the employee does wrestle for them, but that they had no record of him being injured or treated at the facility by the event's doctor. Not to be deterred, my claims person contacted the doctor to verify. The doctor did confirm that the employee was not treated, however, the doctor said that he has a list he keeps of those that refuse treatment so he can protect himself from malpractice suits. In this case, the employee was on it and the doctor noted his match was stopped due to the injury.

This was quite an effort to achieve a claims denial from the insurance company. Think of it this way, stopping at the employee's statement and using just the initial report of the ladder slip causing the injury would have led to the insurance company accepting this injury as a claim. This injury would have most likely cost $20,000-$40,000 in surgical and physical therapy cost and employee wages while off work. Having the fellow employee statement of limping into work was enough evidence for the insurance company adjuster to delay accepting the claim giving the team the time they needed to complete this investigation which took over a week to complete and receive the documentation necessary for the adjuster to issue a denial.

Choosing the Right Broker/Advisor

If you are at the blackjack table and on a losing streak, you are faced with two options: continue to play at that table where you are bleeding chips, or go find another where your luck could change.

As I mentioned in the beginning of this book, many executives, when becoming frustrated with their insurance program, feel that they need to shop their insurance to find relief, or change their proverbial table. What I find even more interesting is that I have yet to find an executive who does not feel just as frustrated by the actual insurance shopping process itself. Let us review that process so you can understand more clearly why looking at a captive is, and should be, a different process to go through.

The Traditional Insurance Process

Face it, somewhere around 90-to-120 days prior to your renewal, the phone calls start. Every agent tells you how great a program they have and how they can save you money. They come in to try to get your policies and your loss runs by saying, "We are going to do a great job for you. We have great insurance company relationships, and we provide great service." In essence, it is very difficult for executives to determine if they really do have the right agent.

I contend that most employers spend less time hiring their agent than they do hiring an employee, when in reality their agent is more likely than an employee to put them out of business.

Agents and insurance companies have conveyed the process as, "This is how you buy insurance. You go out, get a few agents, and get several quotes." Businesses were taught that they should supply copies of their declaration pages from their insurance policies, and three to five years of loss runs. In some cases, the insurance agent will even request a look around their facility, or ask a few questions. Either way, it seems the next time they see that agent is a few days prior to their insurance renewal when they are presenting a quote.

But there are problems with this process. The fundamental flaw with the 90-day submission and bidding process is that it is solely focused on the sale of an insurance product. It is not a thoughtful, detailed, diagnostic system focused on truly identifying and managing your risks.

90 days is not a lot of time:

- Will the agent be able to collect all of the information that they need?
- Will they be able to obtain all the supplemental applications and complete them accurately?
- Will the insurance company accept the application or reject it because another agent applied "first" for a quote from them?
- How well will the agent be able to negotiate with the insurance company?
- Is the insurance company going to be interested in quoting your operations or not?
- Is the insurance company able to provide all the necessary coverage?
- Will the agent prepare a detailed proposal in English as opposed to "insurance-speak"?
- Will the agent ultimately even present you with a quote?
- Will the agent provide all of the coverage you requested, or more importantly, the ones you need?
- Will you have enough time to make a thorough analysis of your options to make sure you make the best decision and nothing is missed?

Many executives mistakenly believe their organization is very attractive to insurance companies because they are inundated with calls from agents offering to quote and save them money. They do not realize that they are attractive to *all agents* because agents receive a commission for selling a product; the bigger the premium, the larger the commission they will make. The issue is these agents still have to sell your company to the insurance companies, who may or may not have any interest in quoting your company or offering you better rates.

There are multiple hurdles, barriers, twists and turns standing in your way. If you are driving down a pothole-filled road there is a good chance you will hit some of them. Since there is a limited amount of time and effort spent in simply trying to get this whole quotation process to work, your critical risk issues may go unaddressed, uncovered, or even worse, unnoticed.

The traditional insurance shopping process is broken. Think of it this way, each of us goes through a process when we go to buy something. It involves identifying, analyzing, controlling, financing or buying, and then using and maintaining the product or service.

For example, if you are going to buy a home, you would not ask several real estate agents to show up at your office, show you printouts of several homes in your metropolitan area that fit your requirements for number of bedrooms and bathrooms, overall size of home and yard; and then sit down and look through the listing sheets and determine which one you buy based on the lowest price of the home. So why would you buy insurance this way?

To buy a home, you are going to invest time and effort in selecting the final home of your choice. You are going to start by identifying the various homes you potentially want to look at and walk through these homes and analyze all of them to determine which one best fits your needs.

But just because you choose a specific home, this does not mean you are done. You are going to figure out how to best control or mitigate any problems by having a home inspection completed to reduce the likelihood of buying a problematic home. Once you know the issues, you can deal with them before you buy, or even choose to walk away.

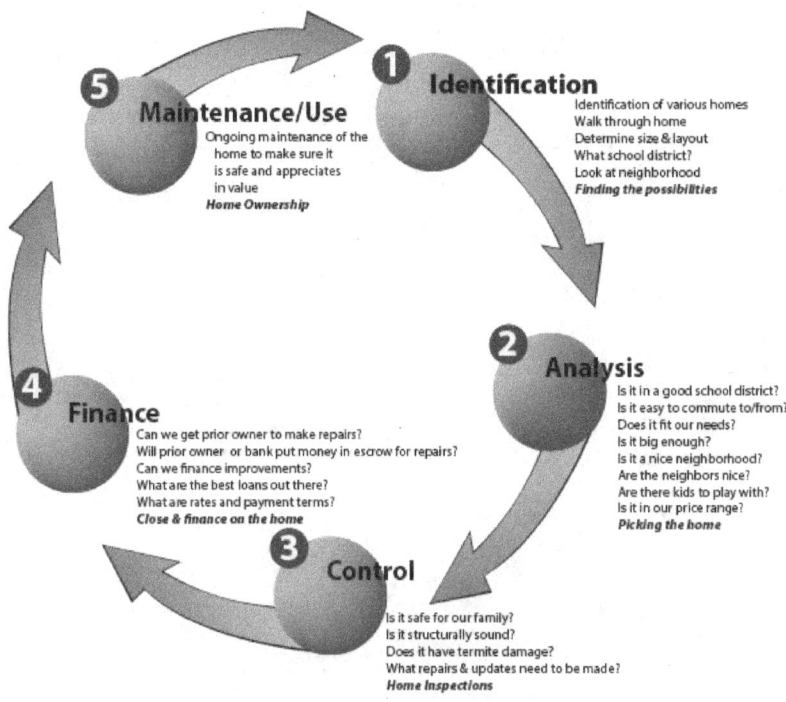

Identification
Identification of various homes
Walk through home
Determine size & layout
What school district?
Look at neighborhood
Finding the possibilities

Maintenance/Use
Ongoing maintenance of the
home to make sure it
is safe and appreciates
in value
Home Ownership

Analysis
Is it in a good school district?
Is it easy to commute to/from?
Does it fit our needs?
Is it big enough?
Is it a nice neighborhood?
Are the neighbors nice?
Are there kids to play with?
Is it in our price range?
Picking the home

Finance
Can we get prior owner to make repairs?
Will prior owner or bank put money in escrow for repairs?
Can we finance improvements?
What are the best loans out there?
What are rates and payment terms?
Close & finance on the home

Control
Is it safe for our family?
Is it structurally sound?
Does it have termite damage?
What repairs & updates need to be made?
Home Inspections

Then you are going to finance the house by searching for the best loan option. You may be prequalified for a total dollar amount you can spend, but you still want to determine which finance program is best for you. Once you decide this, you are going to close and finance the home. Following closing and moving in, you finally get to enjoy the home and take care of the ongoing maintenance so it remains safe and maintains its value.

In comparison, the traditional insurance buying cycle lacks that process of identification, analysis, and control. In the identification phase, the agent gathers copies of your policies and maybe conducts a walk through and obtains loss runs. The analysis phase is spent identifying what they believe are "killer" gaps in coverage and what other policies they can sell to you. The focus of the traditional process is solely on selling you a product.

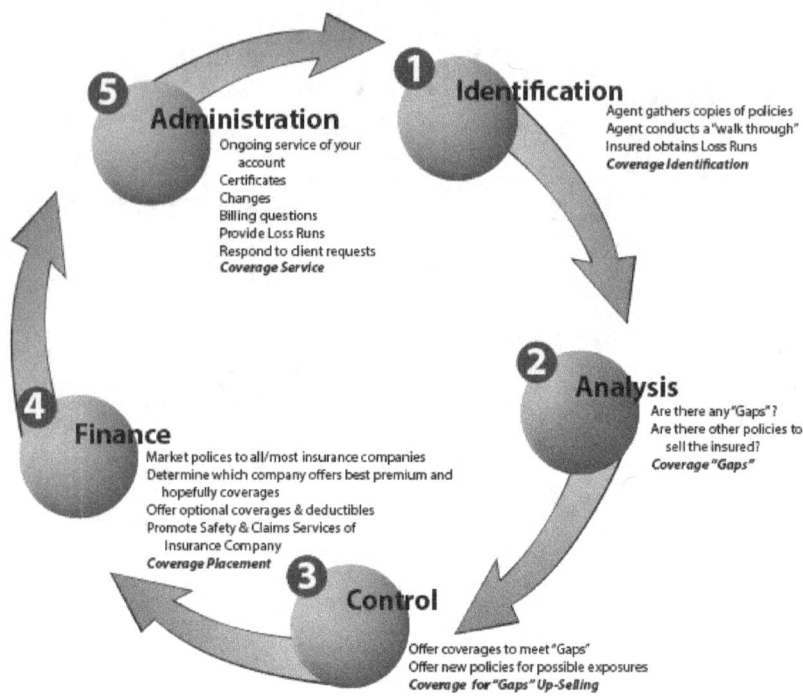

In the control step, they offer coverage to fill those gaps, or offer new policies for possible exposures. In other words, they are looking to up-sell.

In the finance step, they market your policies to all or most of the insurance companies they represent to determine which company offers the best premium and coverage, while also offering options and deductibles to fill those gaps. The agents will then promote the safety and claims services of the insurance company, or they may promote somebody that wears a safety and claims service "hat" in their organization.

For the administration phase, they perform the ongoing service of your account, certificates, changes, billing questions, provide loss runs, and respond to your questions.

As you can see, it is not really a deep identification, analysis, or control that you would have when you purchase a home. It is even worse when you want that "apples–to–apples quote." Basically, the agent goes from gathering the policies and loss runs, then slides all the way over, skipping analysis and control, to the finance phase where they go to market your policies for quotes, determine which company offers the best premium, and then promises the safety and claims services of the insurance company.

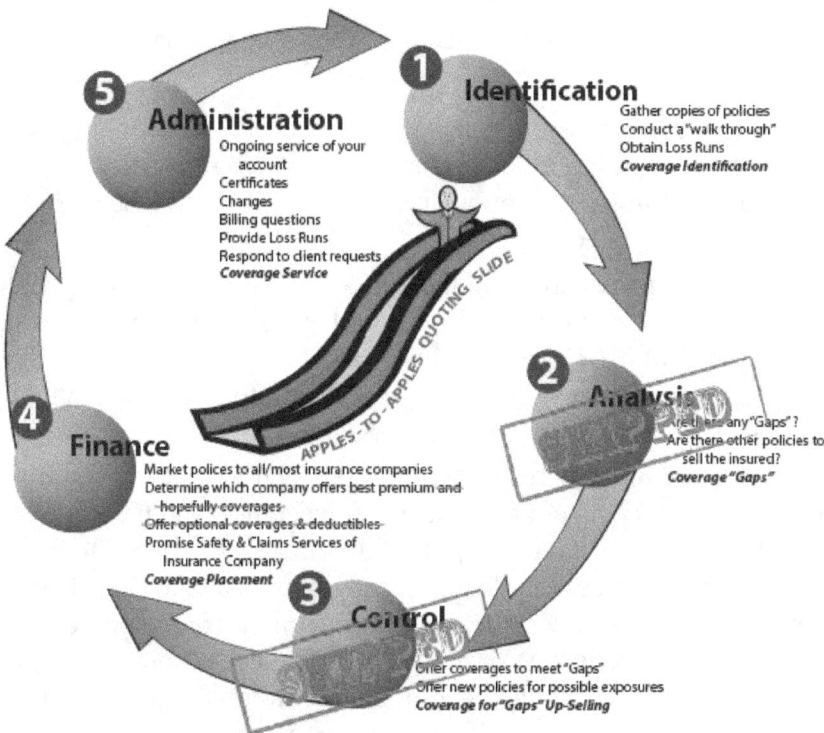

Ultimately, after going through this process most executives I talk to state that they still feel overcharged and also question if they even have the proper coverage or protection.

A Better Process – Choose Your Broker First

Take a step back and look at what you really need to do. You must start back at the identification process and change it to identify first who the right agent or advisor should be. Why not interview the agents and determine and understand what their knowledge, functions and capabilities are?

Ask the agent:

- What is your process of engaging with our company?

- What information do you need, and how do you gather the information you need to provide us with options?
- How do you go about this process?
- What are you and your team's experience and background?

Do not put what you are looking for in your questions because remember, you are talking to a salesperson who will eagerly tell you what you want to hear. You want to find out why they believe it is best to engage with you.

Many executives have told me that they tend to view salespeople as a great source of information because they see what happens inside other organizations: what works and what does not work. However, you must be sure what they do works best for you, so you can understand what expertise the agent brings.

Computers and the Internet have changed how underwriting looks and how underwriting quotes a business' insurance, and the same can be said as to how insurance agents sell policies. There are multiple website-based services that focus on providing insurance agents with information and resources that they can use for marketing purposes in order to attract prospective businesses. These website services allow agents to provide an employer information on topics such as safety, fleet safety, experience modifiers and human resources. However, these website services can also put an employer in the precarious position of trying to determine if an agent is able to provide *information only*, or if the agent truly has the *knowledge* and *experience* to know how best to use that information. These services will make it difficult for you to determine if the agent will be able to properly identify the risks and threats that you are facing and determine the best course of action as a solution, or if they are essentially just throwing marketing materials at the wall with the hope that some of it sticks.

Therefore, you may want to collect resumes or bios on the salesperson and their team. Determine exactly what risk management background and training they have undertaken. One of the biggest frustrations for executives comes from the fact that many of the insurance companies and agents use the term "risk management" to mean loss control. Loss control is when a person visits you, makes a list of physical hazards they see and then wants you to fix them or they will not insure you, or will insure you at a higher premium.

Risk management is much more than loss control. Risk management is an ongoing process of identifying risks; analyzing, measuring and prioritizing them; figuring out how best to control them; and then dealing with the risk transfer and implementation, as well as risk review and refinement. Do not confuse loss control with risk management, even if risk management is in someone's title.

Obtain testimonials and references from satisfied clients. Call them, and find out specifically what they did for them, versus hearing only "they did a great job for us!"

Talk to the agent and find out what processes and programs the agent will implement to help you become a better risk. What insurance companies does the agent represent? First and foremost, never get "happy ears" at the initial answer. Always ask more questions.

For example, I was working with a client looking to identify what agents they may want to work with. While we were sitting together interviewing prospective agents, one agent said that they had a workers' compensation claims person on staff. The owner said, "Great, that will help us."

I proceeded to ask some more questions:

Questions I asked:	Agent's Response:
What process does your claims person play in the injury process?	They take the claim, and report it to the insurance company. They then follow up to make certain that the insurance company provides a claim number to the customer, and if not, gets the claim number and adjuster's name and provides it to the customer.

What do they do after the insurance company provides us with a claim number?	They constantly follow up with the adjuster as to the status of the claim.
How often do they do that?	They do that very often, probably once or twice a week.
Will they contact the business owner during this process?	Yes, they would call the owner periodically to make sure everything is going well from their perspective.
What if it is not going well?	He said that he "guesses" they would follow up with the adjuster and see if they could get the claim back on track.
Anything else?	Not really.

My question to the business owner was what was the agent doing to improve the outcome of claims? What were they doing other than basically chewing up the adjustor's time with really no benefit to you as an organization? It was clear, they were not really adding to the process. They were trying to see where everything was and that was about it.

Included in Appendix A is a section on *Answers to Get Before You Hire a Broker*. Remember, you need to interview this prospective agent as if they were going to be your employee. Take your time. Determine who the best agent would be for you to improve your organization as a risk, and provide the services that you ultimately need that will lead you to improved results and allow the agent you chose to be the one that works for.

And first and foremost, do not do this during the normal 90-day time frame prior to renewal process. Start when there is no pressure to make a buying decision. Taking a look at alternative risk financing and captives should not be a quick decision. Plus, the last thing you want to do is have to make a quick decision, and due to the real fear of making a wrong one under time constraints, you may make the wrong one and deter or delay to the next year. This usually causes you to repeat the same problem again as you may not want to deal with your "insurance" until the next "renewal" as you need to focus on running and growing your company.

In addition to Appendix A, you can also review once again Chapter 11-*Leveraging Risk Management,* which focuses on the risk management process so that you can ask more pointed questions when determining which agent you want to advise you, and ultimately represent you, in the insurance marketplace.

The whole bidding and quoting process with multiple agents going to multiple companies is nothing but a headache. It frustrates employers, frustrates agents, and frustrates insurance companies. In most cases, it can actually make you look less attractive to insurance companies.

Many insurance companies may pass on quoting because they believe there is a lack of control by the business in terms of this shopping process. They see so many agents making submissions to them that they feel they have no real opportunity to be successful.

What is even more concerning, as many underwriters have shared with me, is that underwriters can become uncomfortable in quoting a business when the information they receive from various agents differs from the information provided, and even contradicts the submissions. They may only recognize the agent who first submits an application to them, but they will look at all the information that they receive (as correct or incorrect as that information might be).

In most cases, you will ultimately achieve a better result by determining who would be the best agent/advisor for you in terms of helping your organization achieve your goals and represent your company, and then let them go to the entire insurance marketplace on your behalf. A good rule of thumb: seek first to understand before you seek to act.

If you are still in doubt that the insurance purchasing process is broken, I have one simple question to ask you, *"Have you ever seen what the agent's submission looks like before it is submitted to the insurance company?"*. So how do you know that the agent is positioning you in the best light to get you the best rates and coverage? Most business leaders only see the applications *after* deciding which insurance company/agent to go with and they need to sign them to change companies.

You really should see and understand what the quality of an agent's submission is before it is given to an insurance company, when it becomes part of your permanent computer record. Does the agent actually have a "write-up" or cover letter that conveys a clear story of the quality of your operations, or are they just sending in the industry standard applications and loss runs? What is necessary to make a submission in an effort to simply get a quote or "block the market", is not going to convey how good you are to an underwriter. If you have not seen an agent take photos, or read their cover stories of your operations, you are not going to get the best rates.

You also want to know what insurance companies they are approaching, not because you are trying to assign markets and prevent arguing between who gets what insurance company, you want to know who they are approaching so that you can eventually see the matching response or quote from each insurance company. Similar to Newton's Third Law – *For every action, there is an equal and opposite reaction*, there is my Third Law that states – *For every insurance company submission; there should be an insurance company response (good or bad)*. You need to see the actual physical quote and its details, not just a quote. If they did not quote, you also want to know *why* they specifically did not quote.

A pat response from an insurance company as to why they did not quote is "losses" or "cannot compete." These are usually their first lines of defense when they do not want to take the time and effort to quote your insurance. You need to ask, "Are there certain losses that they are afraid of?" Get specifics. If they said they cannot compete, "What is it from a risk perspective that is keeping the underwriter from using their best rates?". The reason why they usually say they cannot compete is that they are viewing you as such a large risk that they do not want to price aggressively enough to earn your business.

Once when having a pre-submission telephone discussion with an underwriter, I found that they had declined to quote this particular business several times in the past. The underwriter commented that they did not want to quote this business, as there was a particular machine that was old and not guarded properly. Therefore, they were afraid of an employee becoming seriously injured. I did not recall seeing such a machine during my analysis of the facility, and found out from the business owner that the particular machine was replaced four years ago after it broke down. The report the underwriter was using for their decisions was from an inspection performed six years earlier. Because of computers, which have lifetime memory, underwriters will assume nothing has changed unless they are told otherwise, and you will not even get to the step of having loss control come in to see something has changed. This also serves as a reminder as to why it is a good idea to have old recommendations made by the insurance company analyzed.

Without having this conversation and addressing the replaced machine prior to making a submission, the underwriter would have issued a quick declination. Once they issue a declination, it is almost impossible to get an underwriter to reopen a file. Why? **Underwriters do not get in trouble for NOT writing an account, they get in trouble for writing the wrong account.** Underwriting managers can, and will, Monday Morning Quarterback following a large claim and ask the underwriter why they wrote the account, why they quoted it a certain way, and in this case, why they reversed the declination decision.

We already discussed that you would not buy a home just from an agent bringing you a listing. But, would you buy a car without a test drive? Probably not. So why do you buy insurance this way?

So how do you take an insurance agent on a "test drive"? I recommend that you have the agents go through their process to identify risk(s) in your business, how they would specifically help you improve that particular risk(s), and how they would portray you to the insurance company. This is basically your test drive; you would not buy a car without taking a test drive, so I believe you need to take any prospective agent for a test drive.

As discussed before, do not get "happy ears" when they offer lip service like, "Oh, we've got claims services or we have loss control and can help you with your safety." It may sound good, but what risks specifically did they identify? What are they going to do to address those risks? This is simple cause and effect. If the agent cannot convey exactly, in detail, what they identified and what they are going to do for you to address this risk, it clearly means that they do not understand your risks, that they cannot help you improve them, and that they cannot help you leverage the marketplace by showing you are a better risk.

Wrap Up Q & A

Here are the frequently asked questions we receive when discussing captives with business owners:

Q: *"My lenders require my insurance to come from a rated carrier, how can I issue coverage from my captive and still secure my financing?"*

A: For a fee, an A.M. Best rated and licensed insurance company will provide what is known as a "front". The fronting insurance company will be the one listed on certificates of insurance, or on the endorsement, and will satisfy the lender's requirements. Therefore, your lender will most likely not realize you are part of a captive.

Q: *"If I have a catastrophic claim, can I lose all of the money in the captive?"*

A: You decide how much risk you want to retain. Through reinsurance agreements and excess policies, you can tailor your insurance company's exposure to meet your comfort level and objectives. Ultimately, you know going in how much you have exposed for the worst-case scenario, and then the fronting and insurance companies are responsible for the rest.

Q: *"How common are captives?"*

A: Today there are over 7,000 captives worldwide. Over 40% of major U.S. corporations and many of your smartest competitors are involved in captives, such as Verizon and UPS, among others. It is estimated that around 10%-15% of businesses that are paying between $100,000 and $3,000,000 in insurance premiums are in captives. The strongest periods of growth for captives occur as builders respond to hard market insurance environments.

Q: *"Sounds like a lot of work. How much of my company's resources will I need to allocate?"*

A: Your broker and captive manager can provide a turnkey program to design, implement and manage your captive insurance company program. This will allow you to focus on running and growing your company.

Q: *"Do I need an Actuarial or Feasibility Study?"*

A: Absolutely! A study is important because it answers the essential questions; "What will my potential return on investment be by using a captive?", "Does this make financial sense for me to do?". You need to have a clear understanding of what to expect when you invest in a captive.

Q: *"Why are premiums needed as part of my Actuarial or Feasibility Study?"*

A: It is simple, insurance captives are not traditional insurance companies with filed rates, so they cannot state that it will be $1,153 for $1,000,000 of liability and $500 Comprehensive and Collision Deductibles on your 2016 Ford F350 Pickup. They will use actuarial models and your prior claims history to determine your loss fund including the Expected Loss Ratio (ELR) Method, which is the main reason that the captive actuaries *require* your historical premiums. ELR is a technique used to determine the projected amount of claims relative to your historical premiums that the insurance companies collected. Actuaries cannot charge zero premium if you never had any losses, they need to charge some premium for some risk. Plus, if you have less losses than you have allocated to your loss fund, you will receive your potential underwriting profit and investment income as captive dividends are declared.

Q: *"Should I be concerned about risk sharing in a captive?"*

A: Risk sharing is necessary for your captive so that it is viewed as an insurance company, and thus your premiums paid are tax deductible. If there were no risk sharing your captive would be viewed as being self-insurance.

Also, when you really think about it, when you are insured by a traditional insurance company, you are already risk sharing with thousands of other businesses. If the insurance company picks their clients poorly and has too many claims, they will increase future premiums to all members. Your captive will be more selective in choosing members.

The biggest point is that insurance companies also use reinsurance companies as they do not want to pay large, unexpected claims. The reinsurance marketplace allows insurance companies, as well as your captive, to become a stable means of providing insurance coverage to your business.

Q: *"What is contained in the Feasibility Study?"*

A: The focus of the study will depend on the motivating factors for establishing the captive. In general, the feasibility study is a financial and risk management analysis that will always contain the following:

- Assessment of potential risk(s) to be insured
- Actuarial report including premium rates, rating methodology and loss pick
- Analysis of loss reserve requirements
- Information on the fronting insurance company options
- Reinsurance – the insurance company, the per claim and aggregate retention points
- Capitalization and collateral requirements
- Analysis of options for entity structure, domicile
- Expense projections
- Overview of tax considerations
- Five-year prospective financial statements
- Defined dividend and/or profit allocation system

Should you have a question not addressed here or by the book, please feel free to reach out to me. My contact information is in the back of the book in my bio.

Appendices

Appendix A

ANSWERS TO GET BEFORE YOU HIRE A BROKER

When asking your questions, rule number one is to relax and take your time. Remember, do not offer the answer you are looking for in the questioning. Make sure you watch their body language to see if they are comfortable, or struggling to answer. Treat this as an interview, as if you are determining whether or not you will hire this person, just like you would hire an employee.

What would be their process of engaging with your company?

What information do they need, and how would they gather the information they need to provide options?

How would they go about this process?

What is the experience and background of their team, and who have they worked with in the past?

What specific processes or programs will they implement to help reduce our insurance costs?

If they mention Loss Control Services, ask:

1. What services does their prevention person provide?
2. How often will we see their prevention person?
3. What credentials does their loss prevention person have?
4. How long have they been doing this?
5. Are they a dedicated injury prevention person or do they have other duties?
6. How many clients does their prevention person currently work with?

If they mention Claim Services, ask:

1. What involvement will their claims person have with a claim?
2. What type of questions does their claims person ask to determine the severity or validity of a claim?
3. How many claims is their claims person currently handling?
4. Are they a dedicated claims person or do they have other duties?

Other questions:

What is your best practice to make sure our audit is accurate?

What is the best practice to make sure our experience modifier is accurate?

What is the best practice to make sure an injury is mitigated?

How does your process return injured workers in three days or less?

Who typically establishes your panel of physicians?

What criteria are used to determine who is on your panel of physicians?

How would you improve the Risk Profile of our business?

What steps or processes do you go through to do this?

Can you show testimonials, or allow us to call references, that are satisfied with their results? May we see or call them now?

Can you send us a resume or bio for each of your (broker's) team members?

REMEMBER: TAKE A TEST DRIVE! See how well they can identify, analyze and help you improve your Risk Profile and what they truly know about captives!

Appendix B

38 ANSWERS TO GET BEFORE YOU ENTER INTO A CAPTIVE

It is important that you receive a formal proposal from the captive showing you how the captive performs, how you would have performed if you were a member in the prior years, and understand the financial impacts of going into a captive. But you still need to ask questions, lots of them. Here are some for you to ask, but anything that may concern or confuse you, you should certainly ask:

- Domicile- What is the domicile? How many captives are formed there? How long as there been captives domiciled there? What is the political climate of the domicile? How often do you need to meet in the domicile? Where would meetings need to occur?
- Captive Management – Who are the service providers? What is their experience? Are you able to meet with them? How often do you receive financials?
- Group Captive- How many years in existence? How many members? Who controls selection of the members? Can you see the financials of the captive? Can you see the financials of the other members?
- Risk Sharing – How is risk shared between members? How much are you responsible for of your own claims before the other members assist? How is the shared risk calculated?
- Captive in General – What is the expense structure? What are the per claim and aggregate retention levels before reinsurance becomes into play? What is the process to close out program years? What is my maximum assessment for a poor performing year?

- Collateral – What are the collateral requirements calculated? How long would you have to have collateral posted? How many years may have to stack up?
- 831(b) – Who performs the feasibility study? Who does the actuarial analysis? What is the structure of the captive? How is risk pooled or shared? How is policy premium adequacy determined? Has your captive been reviewed by the IRS in the past?
- Group Healthcare Captive – What are the collateral requirements? Is there potential additional premiums assessed due to possible poor performance? What is the claim runoff period? How and when are dividends calculated and paid?
- Expenses – What are the expenses to form the captive? What are the additional costs/expenses to join the captive? What are any ongoing expenses beyond premium payments that may be incurred?

Appendix C

ITEMS REVIEWED AS PART OF A
RISK MANAGEMENT AND HR ASSESSMENT

- Tour of Facility and/or jobsites
- Interview of key employees
- Five Years of Currently Dated Loss Runs (All Insurance Policies)
  - Description of each claim over $10,000
  - Analysis of claims by type, cause, time, from date of hire
- Five Years Premium History
- Five Years of Payroll History
- Four Prior Years of OSHA 300 Logs and 300A Summaries
  - Current Year-to-Date 300 Log
- Three Years of Experience Modifier Worksheets
- BLS Frequency and Severity Rates Industry Comparison
- Injury Reporting & Investigation Forms and Procedures
- Return-to-Work Manual
- List of Physicians Currently Used
- Safety Manuals/Polices & Procedures
- Employee Handbook
- Employment Applications/Packet
- New Hire Procedures
- New Hire Orientation Material and Procedures
- Insurance policies including all endorsements
- Subcontractor/Independent Contractor Agreement
- Certificates of Insurance
- SAFER reports (if you fall under DOT regulations)

ABOUT THE AUTHOR

David R. Leng, CPCU, CIC, CBWA, CWCA, CRM

David R. Leng is the author of the **International Best Seller** - *The Laws of Insurance Attraction,* as well as one of the top selling workers' compensation books for employers, *Stop Being Frustrated & Overcharged (By Your Workers' Compensation Program).* He was awarded the Advisor of the Year for 2008 by the Institute of WorkComp Professionals, and was requested to join the faculty of the Institute of WorkComp Professionals in 2012.

David is a frequent speaker for the Wood Products Manufacturers Association, Hardwood Manufacturers Association, Westmoreland HR Association, the National Workers' Compensation Symposium, SMC Business Councils, as well as other organizations. He has performed over a hundred programs internationally for associations and business groups; and was added to the faculty of the *Institute of WorkComp Professionals* in 2012. He is also a contributing Fellow at the Workers Compensation Institute.

As a 30-year veteran of the Risk Management and Insurance industry and is regarded as one of the brightest minds in the industry due to his unique *Risk Profile Improvement Process*, which identifies, controls and reduces the risk factors inherent in any business that drive costs to an organization's bottom line and hinders a businesses' culture and employee productivity. Since 2004, David has saved his clients well over $50,000,000 in premiums and overcharges.

David is a frequent contributor to *Environmental Health & Safety, Workers' Compensation, Dynamic Business, Construction Executive, Working PArts*, and *HRM Update* magazines, and has been published in a multitude of other periodicals and association newsletters/magazines.

With over 20 years experience specializing in Workplace Culture and Workers' Compensation, is an alumnus of Penn State where he received a Bachelor of Science in Insurance and Risk Management. His professional designations include Certified Insurance Counselor (CIC), Certified Risk Manager (CRM) and Charter Property Casualty Underwriter (CPCU), Certified Benefits & Wellness Advisor

(CBWA), and he's been designated a Certified WorkComp Advisor (CWCA) by the Institute of WorkComp Professionals.

David is also Co-Founder of Keystone CompControl, the nation's largest single network of Workers' Compensation specialists, and is one of only 14 nationwide *Level-5 Advisors* of the Institute of WorkComp Professionals.

David is also Executive Vice President and a Managing Partner of the Duncan Financial Group.

David spends his leisure time boating in the summer and skiing in the winter with his wife, Lynn, and their two children, Alizabeth and Luke. David and Lynn are active members of Emmaus and Autism Speaks, organizations that help support individuals with special needs, including their son Luke, who was diagnosed with Autism at the age of 18 months.

David's hobbies include woodworking and ice hockey, as well as donating considerable time to his local high school by helping to design sets and teaching students how to build them for their musical productions.

You can contact David at (724) 307- LENG (5364), or email at david@davidleng.com.

A journey starts with one step!

— Lao-tzu, Chinese philosopher 604 B.C.

To help you on your journey to slashing your insurance costs and eliminating your frustrations, we would like to provide you with tools and resources you can use to reach your destination.

**Register your book today to receive your
Reader Bonus!**

Visit **TURNINGPREMIUMINTOPROFITS.COM**
to receive these *FREE* resources:

SUBSCRIPTION – receive a complimentary subscription to our monthly *WorkComp Advisory* e-Newsletter full of tips, case studies, and current events that impact managing your operations.

ADMISSION – to Workshops and Webinars designed to provide you with more detailed information on the "how to" of reducing costs, and identifying and managing risks.

RESOURCES –receive resources and tools you need to take control of your insurance program.

CONSULTATION – complete our discovery call questionnaire and receive a 20-minute consultation call to help you get further on your cost reduction journey or help in solving a tricky issue.

RECEIVE ALL OF THE ABOVE *FREE* RESOURCES BY REGISTERING YOUR BOOK AT

www.TurningPremiumIntoProfits.com/CaptiveRegister

WHAT THEY ARE SAYING ABOUT DAVID

David Leng's presentation at the Hardwood Manufacturers Association 2016 National Conference and Expo, **Improving Your Risk Profile to Slash Your Rates,** *provided immediate take-home value to everyone in attendance. The presentation was insightful, well organized and very thorough.*

Members surveyed felt the session responded directly to their dilemma of increasing insurance premiums and decreasing coverage. They walked out the door with ideas for manageable solutions to control their rising premiums.

I personally was impressed that David spent time prior to the session acquainting himself with members of our Association, making sure his material was indeed focused to their needs. It was spot-on.

We will continue to collaborate with David regarding our members' concerns with property insurance and Workers' Compensation costs

Linda Jovanovich, Executive Vice President – Hardwood Manufacturers Association

It was a pleasure to work with David Leng as one of the primary speakers for our recently held Annual Meeting. In addition to being incredibly knowledgeable about what wood products manufacturers require to properly insure their business and manage their risks, David also understands the industry which is critical to helping companies remain in business should they suffer a major loss.

David was well received and has already helped a number of members.

We would be more than happy to have David address our members at a future meeting.

Philip Bibeau, Executive Director – Wood Products Manufactures Association

David Leng's understanding of the intricacies of Workers Compensation is deep and impressive. He helped a packed room of Westmoreland County Chamber members to better understand the challenges (and opportunities) this complicated issue presents to many business owners.

Chad M. Amond, President – Westmoreland County Chamber of Commerce

Working with Duncan we were able to enhance the safety culture in our organization and reduced our Workers' Compensation costs by over $100,000 a year.

Gary Bowser, II, President – Bowser Automotive Group

David Leng is very knowledgeable about Risk Management, Insurance and Workers' Compensation, and a pleasure to work with. His knowledge allowed our company to reduce its premiums by almost 55%.

Mike Spitznagel, CFO – JetNet Corporation

I just cannot thank you enough for helping us to take control of our work comp. In addition to making my life easier by helping to manage our claims, your team helped us create a very strong safety culture. Our injuries are down significantly, but more importantly, you helped reduce our work comp premium by over $80,000 a year.

Lori Bodnar, HR Manager – C Harper Automotive Group

My workers' comp premium was strangling my company's cash flow. I was in a panic, and trying to obtain as many quotes as I could get my hands on to try and reduce my costs. When I first met David, I was about to accept a quote and change insurance companies, during the middle of my insurance policy term, that would save me almost $20,000, which was about 10% of my premium. I allowed David to take a week to analyze my situation, and I was really glad I did!

David saw that if I would have accepted that quote mid-policy year, that my worst claim year would have been on my experience modifier for 4 years and not 3. Costing me almost $35,000.

More incredibly, David found that my experience modifier was WRONG!!!! Not one of the dozen plus agents that I spoke to previously saw that! David was able to get my experience modifier corrected, and my insurance companies had to return over $86,000 to me!

From the analysis, David saw that we also needed to improve our safety programs, hiring processes, and that WE had to better manage our injured employees instead of relying on the insurance company adjuster. David and his team helped us implement all of these changes quickly, and 3 months later, he was able to leverage what he did for us and obtain an insurance policy at our renewal that was over $100,000 lower.

In a span of 4 months, David put almost $200,000 back in my pocket!

Mark S. Duda, President – Duda Cable & Construction

David, you and your team really delivered results! After working with your team for just about a half a year, you dramatically improved the safety of our operation and very quickly reduced our injury frequency. Most importantly, you negotiated with our insurance company and took us from a 15% surcharge to a 15% credit... that's a 30% drop in our rates!!! You gave us an almost $40,000 reduction in our premium!"

Bob Mincin, Owner – Mincin Insulation Services

For more, please visit www.TurningPremiumsIntoProfits.com and click on the Groups/Associations or Client Results tabs

STOP BEING FRUSTRATED & OVERCHARGED
BY DAVID R LENG, CPCU, CIC, CBWA, CWCA, CRM

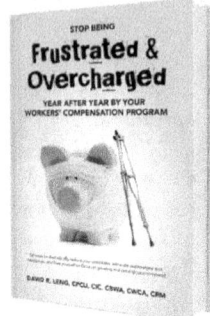

You are not alone in feeling frustrated at the amount of money you have wasted on your workers' compensation program, while wishing you could have put that money to better use elsewhere namely to help grow and run your company.

This book was written to help every business owner, business leader, or executive who has ever been frustrated by the amount of time, energy and money spent dealing with a workers' compensation program that has never achieved the results they were looking for. *Until now.*

Today's technology has both overshadowed and enhanced much of yesterday's craftsmanship.

Now, most of us would definitely not compare a risk manager or an insurance professional to the craftsman who constructed our home or designed that jaw-dropping structure that makes us say "wow."

However, author David Leng aptly ties together a direct correlation between the risk manager and insurance professional to a craftsman. As a business owner, you will see and understand the uniqueness with which David works with his business clients. You will understand how he "builds a fortress" designed to fend off a multitude of employee injuries, view his varying techniques in which to help you appreciate varying Workers' Compensation insurance plans and how insurance companies think about you, then crush and ultimately control your Workers' Compensation insurance costs.

The Institute of WorkComp Professionals has trained many skilled and passionate insurance professionals. With this book, David Leng shows employers how he combines that skill and passion in creating a textbook approach to creating a Workers' Compensation program that actually benefits your company.

Preston Diamond

Preston Diamond
Managing Director
Institute of WorkComp Professionals
Asheville, NC

STOPBEINGFRUSTRATED.COM

As a successful business owner, why would you keep rolling the dice when it comes to managing your insurance program? Constantly frustrating yourself chasing quotes through the broken insurance industry bidding process? Leaving the determination of your premium up to the insurance industry with their "hard" and "soft" market cycles? Only you can answer these questions. But you can take some comfort in knowing that you are not alone.

Nearly 30 years of experience has shown that *the most successful* business owners do not allow their results to be left to chance. They have found that by *better managing their organizations*, they **become more *attractive* to insurance companies and earn significantly lower premiums**. Using these little-known management secrets, they have made their companies more productive, profitable and enjoyable.

Inside these pages, you will find out how to stop gambling as the way to reduce your insurance premiums, and **learn how to put yourself *in a winning position where you ultimately control the game.***

Like any other business owner, I turned to several friends to find out who they were insured with. I was also receiving quite a few calls from agents offering to save me money. Even my agent at that time, who worked for perhaps the largest insurance agency in the region, was trying to find as many options as he could. With so many agents promising they could save me money and deliver results, I thought we would be seeing a substantial reduction. I was wrong.

I was about to take the "best" quote available when a business associate put in contact with David Leng. Because of David's commitment to resolving our situation, we were able to quickly lower our insurance costs. His approach reduced our premium by 41%, in addition to the correcting our premium errors! In two short months, David's program put back over $200,000 in our pocket.

What you will read in this book, is a road map to overcoming high insurance rates, a kind of GPS for lowering your premiums while raising both the productivity and profitability of your company. My situation serves as proof that just getting quotes is not enough to manage your insurance program's costs, that you can do better when you use a better way. I can tell you this from first-hand experience; if you are an employer and don't have David Leng's books in your office, you are putting your company at a serious competitive disadvantage.

Mark Duda, President

Duda Cable Construction, Vandergrift, Pennsylvania

LAWSOFINSURANCEATTRACTION.COM

www.ingramcontent.com/pod-product-compliance
Lightning Source LLC
Chambersburg PA
CBHW071303220526
45468CB00001B/257